The Path to Self-

The Mystical Initiations of Wisdom

KIM MICHAELS

Copyright © 2014 Kim Michaels. All rights reserved. No part of this book may be used, reproduced, translated, electronically stored or transmitted by any means except by written permission from the publisher. A reviewer may quote brief passages in a review.

MORE TO LIFE PUBLISHING

www.morepublish.com

For foreign and translation rights,

contact info@ morepublish.com

ISBN: 978-9949-9215-9-1

Series ISBN: 978-9949-9383-4-6

The information and insights in this book should not be considered as a form of therapy, advice, direction, diagnosis, and/or treatment of any kind. This information is not a substitute for medical, psychological, or other professional advice, counseling and care. All matters pertaining to your individual health should be supervised by a physician or appropriate health-care practitioner. No guarantee is made by the author or the publisher that the practices described in this book will yield successful results for anyone at any time. They are presented for informational purposes only, as the practice and proof rests with the individual.

For more information: *www.ascendedmasterlight.com* and *www.transcendencetoolbox.com*

The Mystical

Initiations

of Wisdom

CONTENTS

Introduction 9
1 | Introducing the Second Ray 11
2 | Introducing Master Lanto 13
3 | Discerning reality from unreality 17
4 | Wisdom and Power 27
5 | I Invoke the Spirit of Lanto 43
6 | Wisdom and Illumination 61
7 | I Invoke Oneness with Lanto 77
8 | Wisdom and Love 95
9 | I Invoke Love-based Motivation 113
10 | Wisdom and Purity 131
11 | I Invoke a Pure Motive for Seeking Wisdom 147
12 | Wisdom and Vision 165
13 | I Invoke an Attitude of Ongoing Victory 181
14 | Wisdom and Peace 201
15 | I Invoke Buddhic Wisdom 215
16 | Wisdom and Freedom 235
17 | I Invoke Freedom in the Spirit 253
2.01: Decree to Apollo and Lumina 271
2.02: Decree to Archangel Jophiel 275
2.03: Decree to Master Lanto 279

INTRODUCTION

This book is part of the series on *The Path to Self-Mastery*. The purpose of the series is to give you a complete course for knowing and passing the mystical initiations of the seven spiritual rays. The books in the series form a progression and it is recommended that you start by working through the book to the First Ray of God Power before progressing to this book.

The purpose of this book is to teach you about the characteristics of the Second Ray, which will show you how to unlock your inner wisdom. If you are new to ascended master teachings, you will benefit greatly from reading the first book in the series, *The Power of Self,* because it gives a general introduction to the spiritual path as it is taught by the ascended masters. This will give you a good foundation for taking greater advantage of the teachings in this book.

This book is designed as a workbook in order to help you better integrate and apply the teachings. You will get the best results if you give the invocation that corresponds to the chapter you are studying. It is recommended that you give a specific invocation once a day for nine days and then study part of the corresponding dictation before or after giving the invocation. Each evening, make calls to be taken to Master Lanto's retreat in the etheric realm over the Grand Teton mountain in Wyoming, United States.

You give an invocation by reading it aloud, thereby invoking high-frequency spiritual energy. For more information about invocations and how to give them, please see the website: *www.transcendencetoolbox.com*. In order to learn more about the ascended masters and how they give dictations, see the website *www.ascendedmasterlight.com*.

1 | INTRODUCING THE SECOND RAY

Color of the Second Ray: Golden yellow
Corresponding chakra: Crown
Elohim of the Second Ray: Apollo and Lumina
Archangel and Archeia of the Second Ray: Jophiel and Christine
Chohan of the Second Ray: Master Lanto
Decrees for the Second Ray: 2.01 Decree to Elohim Apollo, 2.02 Decree to Archangel Jophiel, 2.03 Decree to Lord Lanto (See the back of this book).

Pure qualities of the Second Ray

Traditionally seen as the ray of wisdom, illumination and self-knowledge. At a deeper level, it is the ray that empowers you to see that the separate self is unreal and that separation is an illusion. It is through the Second Ray that you can experience the underlying reality that all life is one because nothing can be separated from the omnipresent Creator. Openness to a higher understanding is also a quality of the Second Ray, as is the realization that there are many valid expressions of truth that all point to the same underlying reality of oneness.

Perversions of the Second Ray

The perversion of the Second Ray is the false wisdom that thinks it knows everything or has an ultimate truth. This illusion is based on the central illusion of duality, namely that "reality" can divided into separate compartments and that the separate mind has the right and the ability to decide what is true and what is untrue. The perversions of the Second Ray can be seen in people who are absolutely sure that they are right – especially those who have become fanatical – and are willing to force others into compliance. Another perversion is intellectualism where people can argue for or against any idea without ever going beyond the idea to a direct experience of the Spirit that is beyond words.

2 | INTRODUCING MASTER LANTO

Have you ever watched one of these movies where they use special lighting and filters to make colors look more radiant and give them a golden overlay? If so, you have a seen a glimpse of what it is like to be in the Presence of Master Lanto or Lord Lanto. His aura is so large and so filled with golden light that you feel like you are in a different world where everything is clear and in which everything is in its rightful place so nothing can disturb the peace. This is indeed how it is.

Master Lanto had several embodiments in ancient China, most notably as the Duke of Chou who is considered the originator of the Chinese wisdom tradition, normally known through the works of Confucius. Lanto ascended in 500 BC and has long since reached the Buddhic level of attainment. During one of his embodiments, he had achieved such a devotion to God that a golden glow was physically visible over the center of his chest, his heart chakra. This has since been expanded so the golden glow covers a size-able area around his etheric form. Once you are inside this radiation, you are indeed in a different world, a world where nothing can be hidden from the penetrating gaze of wisdom's eye, the single eye that sees through all of the smokescreens of the duality consciousness.

Master Lanto has a level of attainment far beyond that required for a Chohan, but he has chosen to serve in this position out of love for his unascended brothers and sisters. It is this love – expressed through the perfect, ever-transcending wisdom of the Second Ray – that will transform those who apply themselves to qualify as Lanto's students.

What does it take to qualify as a student of Master Lanto? Only that you are willing to step back and take a look at your perception filter. Lanto will show us the difference between our personal perception filters and the reality seen through the Flame of Illumination that is anchored in the Royal Teton Retreat, located over the Grand Teton mountain in Wyoming, United States.

This is a unique opportunity, for in seeing how your view of life is colored by your perception filter, you are not left feeling like your are wrong or stupid. In seeing unreality, you also see the reality behind it, which means you see the real you without any filter. You see that your perception filter is simply something you have taken on, and you did so for what seemed to be very solid reasons, seen from the perspective of your past level of consciousness. Given that you now have a higher state of consciousness, why hold on to a perception filter that you clearly see as limited and no longer see as a reflection of who you are?

Master Lanto has unequaled mastery in helping students see through the subtleties of the serpentine logic, the dualistic form of reasoning. He knows this must be a gradual process, and he always takes the long view so characteristic of the ancient wisdom tradition. Because he has reached Buddhic attainment, time is no longer a factor for Lanto so he has infinite patience with his students.

If you come to him with a desire to defend or justify your ego and seek to convince Lanto through serpentine logic, he will patiently listen to you for as long as you keep projecting upon him. You will find no response, other than a gentle smile that often provokes the ego more than any worded rebuke. As you continue to project the serpentine logic, it is inevitable that you will eventually get yourself into a logical blind alley where you reach the state that makes you open to Lanto's guidance: confusion.

Once you make a shift and now decide that you want him to help you escape your philosophical catch-22, Lanto will guide you according to your level of attainment and your willingness to see beyond duality. Once you stop seeking to hide, you will find his guidance penetrating, but always unconditionally loving. As Master Lanto sees through all of the conditions defined by the serpentine mind, he also accepts no conditions as a substitute for the real you.

Always supporting the real you, students eventually realize that Lanto sees something in them that they cannot see. When you form a true desire to see yourself through Lanto's eyes, you will discover not wisdom, but the infinite, unconditional love that is beyond but flows through all of the seven rays. That is when you will see a sparkle in Lanto's eyes, and his smile will change from the more impersonal Buddhic variant to a very personal smile of welcoming and approval.

3 | DISCERNING REALITY FROM UNREALITY

Master Lanto I am, and I am the Chohan of the Second Ray. The Second Ray has often been seen as the ray of God's wisdom. When I say God Wisdom, how many people focus on the word "wisdom" and forget the word "God?" They think wisdom means the worldly wisdom, for what frame of reference do they have for even envisioning God Wisdom? Many people have taken onto themselves a graven image of God, and even if they did consider a wisdom that is beyond the worldly wisdom, what they would look at would be the wisdom that they attribute to the false image of God, the image they have been worshiping now for centuries and millennia and even beyond recorded history.

It could be said, indeed, that the essential problem on earth is the false image of God that people have had since the original fallen angels first descended to this earth. They spread their own graven image of the external deity, in whatever form they used that appealed to the people of the time.

How can you know God Wisdom if you do not even know God, if you think that God can be fit into a little mental box created here on earth, or created beyond the earth by the fallen beings who thought they knew better than God how to run a universe? I can assure you that had the fallen angels been put in charge of running the universe, that universe would long ago have self-destructed through the mechanism that we have described as the second law of thermodynamics. There is a force that breaks down any system that contains internal contradictions because it is based on the false wisdom created through the duality consciousness; what we have also called the serpentine mind.

A special invitation to the Royal Teton Retreat

As the Chohan of the Second Ray, I come to offer you that if you will give the invocations in this book, you will be invited to come to the Royal Teton Retreat for a special session. This will help those who are ready, those who are willing, to see through the serpentine wisdom, to see through the mechanism whereby beings who have entered behind the veil of duality think they can create their own definition of wisdom. You will gradually, according to your own level of consciousness, be tutored in how you can free your mind from the many subtle ideas that have been put into the collective consciousness by the fallen beings in their attempt to snare humankind in the most common belief you find on earth. This is the belief that: "We have an absolute truth. We know what is real, we know what is true, we know whether there is a God and what that God is like." He is as described in our religion. Or he is *not* according to our religion of materialism.

This is a special offer to those who are willing to give the invocations in this book and then ask before you go to sleep to be taken to the Royal Teton Retreat, which is located over the Teton mountain range in the United States, in the state of Wyoming. The tallest of these peaks is called the Grand Teton, and it is here you find the golden doors that open up to our retreat.

We have in the past described these doors as huge bronze doors, but through the alchemy of the spirit and the attendance of so many spiritual people on earth, we have upgraded these doors to being pure gold.

We want to signal to all who come to our retreat that behind it you will find the Golden Illumination Flame that burns brightly on the altar in the central hall of our retreat. You might picture it as a vast space with a huge dome above it, far bigger than the domes you see on earth in famous buildings around the world. This is a dome that is not held up by columns, but that is held up by shafts of light that have taken on such intensity that they can carry the dome. The dome is made, of course, not of physical substance but is still made of a substance that is denser than the light that is holding it up.

The light holds up the material universe

This is a symbol of the fact that everything is upheld by light. Everything that is manifest as a visible substance in the material universe is truly hovering on a foundation of light. There is an old joke that an Eastern master once said that the entire material universe rests on the back of a turtle, and then he was asked: "Well, what is underneath the turtle?" His answer was: "It's turtles all the way down." Of course, this was meant in the joking tradition of the Zen Buddhists who seek to confound the linear mind. There is no such thing as a turtle upholding the universe, but there *is* light upholding the material universe, and it is indeed light all the way up or down. Whichever direction you go, you end up at the Creator's Being.

The real goal of coming to the Royal Teton Retreat is twofold. First, it is to confound the intellectual linear mind – the analytical mind – that desperately wants to know everything, that desperately wants to be able to put every aspect of life, every aspect of God, into its database. It wants to fit everything it encounters into some category where it can be assigned a certain label in the database. This is the eternal goal of the analytical mind, for only then does it feel it has done its job. Only then can the ego feel that it has you and your life under control—for you have accepted a label for yourself.

The first goal of coming to the Royal Teton Retreat is that we help you shatter these labels that you put on yourself, put on God, put on every aspect of life in the material realm. We help you see that it is possible to go beyond, that it is possible to go beyond the limitations that human beings have put upon themselves for eons. They have been reinforced in the collective consciousness so that there are many people today who even will not believe that when Christ walked the earth he performed miracles that cannot be performed according to the so-called laws of nature. Or they will not believe that when I walked the earth in my last embodiment, it was possible to see the radiation of my threefold flame through the physical flesh.

Many people in today's world will immediately reject such ideas, and it is a clear proof of how the collective consciousness has been polluted by these limiting beliefs that put down the power of God within you. As Jesus said: "With men this is impossible, but not with God, for with God all things are possible." *All things are possible!*

What you can envision and accept, can be manifest as a physical manifestation. The mother light, the Ma–ter light, will outpicture any image projected upon it with sufficient intensity. What you see today in the material realm is nothing but an image projected by the collective consciousness. What you see on earth is projected by the collective consciousness of the inhabitants of the earth, past and present. When you project a different image, the outer manifestations will change according to the cycles of the four levels of the material universe.

God Wisdom is not intellectual

What is the point of giving you wisdom that satisfies your intellect and makes you feel that you are an advanced spiritual student, if it does nothing to challenge the limitations that you have accepted for yourself? Do you think that we, who are the spiritual teachers of humankind, sit there and pour worldly wisdom upon our students so they become wiser and wiser in the worldly sense? Do you not realize that we have been teachers for a very long time, some of us having ascended centuries ago. We have seen countless students both while we were in embodiment and after. We have seen how they come, how they want wisdom, how they want to be thought wise among men. They look to the ascended masters to give them wisdom so that they can go out and satisfy their egos' need for validation and feel they are somehow better than others.

Of course, we welcome all students, especially at the Royal Teton Retreat, which is one of the initiatic retreats where people come first when they are ready for some kind of higher teaching. We must satisfy whatever desires the students have when they first come. What we look for are those who have come to the point where they are willing to recognize the limitations of worldly wisdom. They are willing to see that there must be something more than always intellectualizing and philosophizing about this or that aspect of cosmic law or this or that aspect of the spiritual realm. When a student comes to that level, then we offer them a higher path in our retreat where they can go beyond. They gradually begin to realize, that the second purpose, the real purpose, of coming to the Royal Teton Retreat is to touch the hem of the Golden Cape of Illumination, which is the Flame of Illumination, and it is an energy, a vibration that is beyond anything on earth.

Teaching a neophyte student at the Royal Teton

If we took neophyte students and brought them into that central hall where the Illumination Flame burns, then they would be burned. Their sense of having everything under control would be shattered to the point where they would go through a severe identity crisis. We do not allow beginning students to come in contact with the flame. We do not allow them to even enter the hall that contains the flame until they are ready for this. They have demonstrated the willingness to let go of their intellectual, philosophical ideas, to question all of the beliefs that they have and to do so without losing their sense of identity, without losing their foundation in life.

When they demonstrate this willingness, then we will let them into the hall. In the beginning, they will sit along the walls of this hall, they will sit on their seats and they will watch the flame at a distance. They will simply sit there and look from a distance and gradually get accustomed to the vibration of this Golden Illumination's Flame. After a time measured individually by each student's ability and willingness, then they might move closer. They might gradually move closer and closer until they will be able to walk up to the round enclosure that surrounds the pedestal from which the flame burns.

The golden plume in the threefold flame of your heart

They will be able to kneel almost within touching distance of the flame. They will be able to absorb the Golden Illumination's Flame in gradually increasing intensity until that flame leaps from the pedestal into their heart, into the secret chamber of their heart, where it now becomes the very golden plume in the threefold flame. This is when you are one of the students of Christ that can rightly divide the Word of Truth, knowing what is real and unreal simply by comparing everything you encounter on earth to the vibration of the Golden Illumination's Flame in the secret chamber of your heart. This is the ultimate measure for what is real and unreal—not even what is true and untrue. This is a concept that has been so misused by the serpentine mind that it has almost become meaningless.

There *is* something that is real and that is the Flame of Illumination. By having that Flame of Illumination as your frame of reference, because it is anchored in your own heart center, you can know what is not real because it is not that flame, it is not vibrating with that flame. The goal we look for at the Royal Teton Retreat is to raise up students to the point where they have the Golden Flame of Illumination anchored in their hearts so they can go out and bring that illumination to society. They can help bring forth the Golden Age of Saint Germain, which truly must be built on the ability to distinguish between the false wisdom of the serpentine mind and the true wisdom and illumination of the Flame of God. I, Lanto, have for centuries supported my beloved brother Saint Germain and his efforts to bring forth the golden age on earth. We are closer than ever, but we are only as close as the students in embodiment are willing to embody the Flame of Golden Illumination and the other flames of the other rays.

I have given you this glimpse of the initiations to which you can aspire. I assure you that the decrees to the Second Ray and the invocations in this book form the best tools available in the physical octave for tuning in to the Second Ray and the Golden Flame of Illumination. They are also the best way of making sure that you can travel to the Royal Teton Retreat every night and that you can partake in these initiations. Through these decrees and invocations, you can gradually build up the momentum that makes it possible for you to carry that Golden Flame of Illumination into the material realm so that your physical body and your outer mind can even withstand having that vibration in the secret chamber of your heart.

I, Lanto, give you this golden opportunity, and we shall see your willingness to multiply the talents given and the willingness of people around the world to tune in to this momentum, created by those who are willing to give these calls to the Second Ray and to the other rays.

A major dispensation to transcend old momentums

By releasing these decrees and invocations to all of the seven rays, we give you a major dispensation, a major opportunity for the spiritual people on earth to transcend their old momentums. You may think our decrees and invocations look simple, even simplistic. Some have called them nursery rhymes, but I tell you, as with everything else, we have done our part to give you a tool. The effectiveness of that tool cannot be guaranteed in the realm of free will. We *can* guarantee that the tool will work according to your willingness to multiply the talents. It is up to you, all of the spiritual people on earth, how well you will make use of this tool and how much we can multiply based on your own multiplication of the original impetus given.

There is indeed a potential that if enough people take up these decrees and invocations to the seven rays, we can see a major breakthrough. We will suddenly have people in embodiment who represent each of the seven rays and even the Eighth Ray of integration. Humankind will truly be able to bring forth a new approach to all of the problems you see on earth, based on having that frame of reference of each of the rays being able to empower people to transcend specific problems that are created out of the perversions of the rays.

Nothing in the material universe can be created without the seven rays, which means that no limitation can be generated without it being a perversion of one of the seven rays. When people in embodiment invoke the pure light of a particular ray, that light will consume the perversions. The characteristics of the ray will give people the insight that they need in order to transcend the belief that created the perversion. Once the misqualified energy and the misqualified belief have been transcended, then the problem will be no more. People will be able to bring forth the true manifestation of that ray, and suddenly you will begin to see major progress in society.

These years after 2012 can be looked at as a new opportunity, as a clean sheet, as a fresh new start for humanity. There is a major potential for building the foundation for a golden age. This must start with some students being willing to transcend their old momentums on each of the seven rays so that they can come to that point of being the open door. This is the opportunity you have by using this and the other books in the series. I say: Be sealed in the Golden Flame of Illumination that I, Lanto, hold for the earth, the Golden Flame of Illumination that I AM.

4 | WISDOM AND POWER

I AM the Ascended Master Lanto. I have been known as Lord Lanto. I am indeed the Lord or the Chohan of the Second Ray of God Wisdom; yet, I prefer not to use the word "lord" because it has been so misused by both secular and certain religious movements on earth. I am not an overlord of you. I do not see *you* as you see yourself. I do not see *me* as *you* see me.

I have been an ascended master for a very long time as measured with earth time, although it is still in the blink of an eye of cosmic time. I consider myself somewhat of a newcomer in the ascended realm, but as measured with earth time, it *is* a long time. I have, therefore, ascended to the Buddhic level of consciousness, and as such, I see the reality taught by Gautama that everything is the Buddha Nature.

I see the Buddha Nature in myself, and in seeing the Buddha Nature in myself, I see the Buddha Nature in *you,* even if you do not yet see this. It is therefore my goal, my only goal, to awaken you to the point where you *can* see the Buddha Nature in yourself, the Buddha Nature in everything that surrounds you, and even see the Buddha Nature in *me* so that you will know that we are indeed equals, as all self-aware beings are equals in the reality of the light of the Wisdom of God.

Ultimate wisdom

What is ultimate wisdom? Consider how men have been striving for wisdom for ages, but the ultimate wisdom is that all life is one, that all is the Buddha Nature, and thus, differentiation in form does not mean differentiation in value. Value, then, being a wholly artificial concept created by the mind that has separated itself from the reality of wisdom, that has created the illusion that it is separated from the Buddha Nature, that the Buddha Nature is not where it is, that the separate mind has created a separate abode that has somehow shut out the Buddha Nature.

There will a come a point in your own growth where you will see how ridiculous the claim is that something could be set apart from the Buddha Nature. You will see that the Buddha Nature is all and in all, and that without him was not anything made that was made. Nothing can be set aside from that which is everywhere, which is unconditional, which is all-penetrating. Yet, I fully understand that as you come to my retreat on your journey from the 48th to the 96th level of consciousness, you will not be able to see this. You will not be able to experience it, and why not? Because you are still looking at life through the perception filter that corresponds to the level of consciousness where you are at, and this is, of course, as it should be.

Shed the perception filters of anti-wisdom

My role as a teacher is to help you penetrate the veils of anti-wisdom, the veils created by the separate mind, the dualistic mind, the serpentine mind, the fallen mind—whatever you want to call it. Of course, we who are ascended only use these words because we know that, while you are yet on earth and see things through the linear mind, you need a name. Labels truly come from the mind of separation. We then do not need to label, for we experience the reality of the Buddha Nature, the one mind.

We instantly feel when something is separate from it. To us, all that is separate is, in a sense, like darkness. It is all unreal; it is all something you need to overcome. For us, it is not a matter of creating gradations, value judgments of saying that one kind of darkness is better than another kind of darkness. They are both unreal. They both need to be left behind as the illusions they are.

This is our role. In order to play that role, we do need to go in and look at you, look at your state of mind, look at your particular perception filter, look at the core beliefs that make up your perception filter, and then we need to address those beliefs. When you come to a certain level of consciousness, you are seeing life through a perception filter; yet, may I take this one step further? May I suggest that, as you climb from the 48th to the 96th level of consciousness, you are shedding a particular perception filter, a particular layer of perception filter, for every step you climb.

While you are at the 48th level, you are looking at life through 48 perception filters. Each of these 48 filters represents one step up the spiral staircase of initiation that leads you from the 48th to the 96th level of consciousness. I am not thereby saying that you are free from perception filters at the 96th level. You then start another level, another layer, of working through the 48 perception filters between the 96th and the 144th level.

It is helpful for you to know, and you will certainly learn when you come to my retreat, that the role, the process, you are going through, is to shed one perception filter at a time. This will help you understand that, when you are at a certain level of consciousness, you cannot instantly shed all of the perception filters through which you are looking at life. You may have 40 perception filters left that you are looking through. You cannot shed all forty at once. If this were to happen, you would lose your sense of identity, you would lose your bearings, you would lose your sense of continuity, you would lose your sense of self. You cannot instantly shift from a very human sense of self to the sense of self based on the individuality anchored in your I AM Presence. This would not be possible; you must take one step at a time, shed one perception filter at a time.

This can give you a sense of patience, as Jesus said: "In your patience possess ye your souls." When a new student comes to my retreat in order to begin the process of ascending under the tutelage of the Second Ray, then that student often is somewhat impatient. This is natural, for you have just passed the initiations, the seven layers of initiations, under the direction of my beloved Master MORE and the first ray of God Power and Will. You need to develop a certain will, a certain determination, you need to have a certain power in order to pass those initiations. It is both natural and right, but one of the most important insights you can come to about the spiritual path is that it has certain stages. What will get you through one stage, will not get you through the next stage.

The challenge at the retreat of the Second Ray

I have many students who come to the Royal Teton Retreat, and they think they can *power* their way through the initiations of the Second Ray. They have worked up a momentum on the First Ray, they think they have this power figured out. They think that it is just a matter of using their power, their drive, their momentum, their determination, to go in and study and study until they find this secret book, this secret insight, the secret wisdom, that will now propel them to the mastery of the Second Ray. Ah, my beloved, this is indeed a challenge for me. In a sense, such students are what we all want. They are eager to learn, they are eager to make progress; yet in their eagerness they are making it so much harder for themselves to make progress, especially on the Second Ray of God Wisdom.

The greatest challenge that we face as ascended masters is that we have ascended. We have shed the perception filters that people have on earth. We have risen to a higher stage of consciousness. We face a very delicate challenge when we help you go through the same process, arising to our level of consciousness.

The challenge is that we cannot give you an accurate view of the difference between your state of consciousness and the ascended state of consciousness. You simply cannot fathom what the ascended state of consciousness is like as you look at life through your many perception filters. We cannot even give you an accurate view of the difference, the distance, between the unascended and the ascended state of consciousness. If we were to convey this to you, you would be discouraged. You would think it was almost hopeless because the distance is so great that it seems impossible to cross it.

It is, of course, not impossible, but it is, indeed, an absolutely incredible transformation that you go through from the lower levels of human consciousness to the ascended state of consciousness. Imagine, as a linear illustration, that you have two people who were both blind from birth. Suddenly, one person is given sight and now sees the world as you see it. Imagine that this person was to describe to the other person what the world now looks like.

Imagine that you had to describe what the world looks like to a person who had been blind from birth and had never seen what you see and what you take for granted. It is such a gap between the ascended and the unascended state of consciousness that there are no words that we can use to describe the difference in a way that you can understand.

How ascended masters communicate

You are hearing or reading the words that are originating with me in the ascended realm. You may think that I am somehow standing up here in a higher realm, or perhaps sitting up here in a higher realm, and I am speaking words that the messenger is then receiving and giving physical expression through his voice. This is not the case. I am not sitting up here speaking words, for in the ascended realm we do not communicate through words. We communicate in a way that is so different that you can barely fathom it in the unascended state. One could say that we communicate through thoughts, but that is not accurate either because your thoughts are so different from the way we think.

We communicate in a way that is holistic and all-encompassing. We are not just communicating through ideas, but through feelings, sensations, experiences. As I am giving this dictation, I am, indeed, manifesting my Presence in a certain location in the lower spiritual and higher etheric realm. I am concentrating my essence, my mind essence, in a certain "location" as you might call it. I am expressing an impulse that can be directed into the four levels of the material universe, the identity, mental, emotional, and physical. I am then directing that impulse into the four levels of the mind of the messenger where it is working its way down through his identity, mental and emotional body until it reaches the level of the conscious mind where it is expressed as the words that you hear or read. The clothing of words takes place in the four levels of the material realm because what I am sending out is not words but a holistic form of communication.

Reach for the deeper essence behind the words

You are so used to, you are so programmed to, expect that communication takes place in the form of words. The biggest challenge I face is that I have to speak in words that you can hear or read, for otherwise you cannot grasp any impulse from my level of consciousness. What I am seeking to communicate to you is not actually the words or the meaning that the linear mind attaches to those words. What I am seeking to communicate to you is an *experience,* a glimpse, of the holistic communication that I am projecting from my level of consciousness towards yours.

It is this inner, mystical, holistic experience that will transform your consciousness; not the words and not the meaning. You may think it is meaningless to say with words that you should not pay attention to the words; yet, I am not actually saying that you should not pay attention to the words or the meaning. What I *am* saying is that you should not pay *exclusive* attention to the words and their meaning. You should have a part of your attention on seeking to go beyond the words so that you may experience, even if only in a brief glimpse, the all-encompassing holistic nature of my communication.

A major purpose of this series of books is to give you the tools whereby you can grasp enough of the qualities of a particular ray with your outer mind that you are actually able to tune in to that ray so that, when your mind leaves the body during sleep, you can travel to our etheric retreats. You need to understand that when you do go out of your body, and take note that I am not being very specific when I say "you," then you take with you your perception filters. This means that when you come to an etheric retreat, you expect to find something there that is familiar to what you know from earth.

Do you begin to glimpse the challenge that we face? Our task is to help you go beyond your perception filter, but when you come to us as a student, you come with your perception filter, and you expect that we will, to some degree, validate your perception of life. When you come to a certain level of consciousness, such as the 58th level of consciousness, we cannot shatter all the perception filters. It is not our job at that level to shatter all of them, but only to help you go beyond the one that corresponds to that level so that you can take the next step up.

When you come to our retreats, we are ready to help you shed the perception filter that corresponds to your current level of consciousness, but the big question is: "Are *you* ready to let go of that perception filter?" This is the all-important question, and I bring this up as my first level of instruction because it actually determines whether you can even enter the Royal Teton Retreat and begin instructions under me.

Wisdom is not a weapon

There is a certain percentage of students that get stuck in a kind of no-mans-land. They have passed the initiations of the First Ray, but they have become so over-enthusiastic about the application of power that they cannot make the shift into the initiations of the Second Ray. They want to come in and power their way through wisdom, through the initiations of the Second Ray. They come much like you see many students in the universities of the world where they think that, if they just study and fill their minds and program their minds with all this wisdom – this knowledge, this ability to remember or recite by heart – then they will pass the exam. That is not the way it works in the retreat of the Second Ray.

God Wisdom is not worldly wisdom. If you come to the initiations of Divine Wisdom while projecting an image of worldly wisdom, you cannot truly engage these initiations. That is why the first step we must take people through is to actually help them shed the perception filter that is so prevalent in the world, the perception filter where people think that wisdom should be used as a weapon.

Unfortunately, quite a few students have had this perception filter reinforced as they went through the initiations of the First Ray. Master MORE is well aware of this. He seeks to do everything he can to help people avoid reinforcing the perception filter of the misuse of wisdom, but his options are limited because at the 48th or the 52nd level, you are not ready to shed that perception filter. You are not ready until you come to the Second Ray and the first level of initiation under the Second Ray.

Master MORE cannot truly take you through that initiation. He knows that you have this perception filter. He can only seek to help you not to reinforce it, but some students do not hear him. They do use the power, the momentum, that they gain during the initiations of the First Ray to reinforce the perception filter. They now come into my retreat, and they expect that they can find some wisdom, they can study so hard, that now they become better, wiser, smarter, more knowledgeable than other students.

They do as you see many people in the world do. They do what you see the intellectuals do all the time where they have debates that turn into a kind of competition to see who has the most wisdom, who can outsmart and outmaneuver others. Surely, there *must* be an opposition, there must be something that is *true* and something that is *false*. Those who know what is true must overpower those who do not have the same knowledge, who do not have the same way of looking at life, and therefore, must be wrong, false, of the devil. They must be deceivers. They must be out to fool and manipulate others, and we must overpower them with our wisdom.

Words are tools for transcendence

This is what you see in the world. It is a very common reaction, is it not? Perhaps you will even recognize that you, or at least people you know in the spiritual field, have engaged in this seeking to overpower others? How many of you believe that your spiritual knowledge, whether it comes from the ascended masters or some other teaching or teacher, is superior to all others? Again, we have a challenge faced by your ascended teachers.

I am not here saying that the wisdom we are giving you is not true, is not correct, is not valid, but it is not ultimate wisdom, for ultimate wisdom is beyond words. It is holistic, it is all-encompassing, it is an experience. What I give you, what we give you through our teachings, is only words and in the translation into words, the all-encompassing, holistic nature is somewhat lost. This does not mean that the words are not valuable, but they are only tools for transcendence. When you take a worded expression, be it the Bible or an ascended master dictation, and turn it into an absolute truth, then you have lost wisdom, Divine Wisdom. You have gained worldly or human wisdom, but that is a poor substitute for the real thing. This is what you need to start recognizing at the first level of initiation in the Royal Teton Retreat.

The first initiation at the Royal Teton Retreat

We take students and we put them together in groups and we ask them to debate a specific question. At first, we simply ask them to debate based on what they already know. One question, for example, is: "How can human beings know anything? How can you know that what you know is real, is true, is valid?" This is a question that philosophers have been debating for centuries. You might benefit from studying a little bit of philosophy and see what philosophers have said about it because this is precisely what you will do at the first level of my retreat.

After students have had their first debates based on the knowledge they have with them, we ask them to go into our libraries and look at how the world's philosophers have dealt with that particular question. We then ask them to each pick a philosopher, and then they come together and they argue the issue based on what particular philosophers have said about it.

Then, we ask them to continue this debate. We give them no directions, no help. They, of course, throw themselves at this task very eagerly, and the people who have taken their momentum of power and transferred it to wisdom are the most eager ones.

They pick a philosopher and they believe that this philosopher had the right view, he had the *only* truth. Then, they continue to argue based on his truth, as if his truth really was the highest possible way to look at the issue, as if it really was an absolute truth. They argue against the others, but the others also have the view that *their* philosopher had the highest truth so they sit there, and they gradually form factions. In many cases, they start out with a number of viewpoints that gradually get eliminated, and it boils down to there being two main opponents.

You will see, if you look at philosophy, that for almost every issue there are two main schools of thought. One is the Father, one is the Mother; one is a perversion of the Father and one is a perversion of the Mother; the expanding and the contracting forces. We then let them argue for as long as it takes, and I can tell you that it is good that we who are the instructors at the Royal Teton Retreat have reached a Buddhic level of attainment.

It is amazing how long students can sit and argue before they come to the point where they start thinking that since no side can convince the other side that it is right, perhaps it is necessary to find a different approach to the issue. When a student begins to question the debate itself, the mindset itself, then *that* student is ready to move on.

We will sometimes start out with a large group of students. We are letting them debate, taking turns presenting their viewpoints, and we are simply watching. When a student begins to question the debate itself and the mindset behind the debate, *then* we can pull that student out. A student can then move on to the next level, which is no longer the initiation of wisdom expressed through power, but the expression of wisdom through the Second Ray of wisdom itself.

Students who do not pass the first initiation

The students who have not started questioning the debate, we leave them to continue debating. It often takes a long time, but gradually, students are pulled out, and in many cases, it ends up with only two students remaining. They are the ones who became the leaders, the ones who had the most power in their expression of wisdom, the ones who were the most convinced that they were right, that there had to be only one truth. They would, therefore, argue their case with great power.

You will be amazed at how long such powerful students can keep arguing against each other. You will be amazed how they can keep going into the libraries, pouring over books seeking to find the ultimate argument. It has, indeed, happened that students have come to a point where they could not let go and where they became so angry at their opponent that they had to leave, not only our retreat but the process of initiation.

Some people have fallen down to the corresponding level below the 48th level because they would not give up the attempt to overpower the opposing side with their wisdom. This is not something that happens often, but it is a possibility because you can, at every stage between the 48th and the 96th level, fall down to the corresponding level below the 48th level. This happens when you pervert the initiation of your current level of consciousness through anger or fear or other negative emotions. You continue to express it in more and more extreme forms without being willing to question whether there is another way, whether there is a way that does not lead to frustration.

I would like you to know that, if you look at public life on earth, you can see that there are such people in today's world. You will find them in the media, in the political arena and in the area of science and educational institutions, such as universities. These people love to debate others in an intellectual way. They often think they have great knowledge and wisdom, but it is worldly wisdom, it is dualistic wisdom. It can never lead to a resolution. I can tell you that some of the people today that you see writing books about a specific topic have been doing this for a very long time. They may be writing books that argue against a particular viewpoint, but this is not something that started in this lifetime. It started lifetimes ago.

There are people in embodiment today in intellectual circles who were embodied as the Scribes and Pharisees 2,000 years ago. Back then, they used their worldly wisdom to argue against Jesus when he stood before them as the Living Christ. There are some in embodiment today who are among the Brahmins of the Hindu religion that argued against Gautama when he appeared before them in the flesh. They argued why the Buddha could not be right when he said that everything was the Buddha Nature, for this contradicted the scriptures they had at the time, and they used great intellectual skill and vigor to argue against it.

Experiencing the Spirit of Wisdom

This is the pattern of abusing wisdom with power. You elevate one expression with words as a superior form of wisdom, and now you project upon everything that it must conform to this wisdom. You even project on the Living Buddha and the Living Christ that he or she must conform to your perception filter. The Living Buddha and the Living Christ have come to help you escape the closed mental box of your perception filter. The box is closed because you have taken one statement of wisdom and you have applied power to elevate it to the status of being absolute. Your statement of wisdom may be perfectly valid. It may be true, but it is not the *only* way to describe reality. It is not the *only truth,* for there is no one and only truth. Any worded expression is just one description. It does not mean that they are all true or all equally valid. There are worded descriptions that are false, but there is more than one that is true, valid, real and useful. They are all only *that;* they are only *descriptions* that can be useful for transcending the words and gaining the holistic experience of the Spirit of Wisdom, the spirit that is the originator of the Word but that is more than the words, that is more than the form.

Ah, my beloved, here is the difference between those who pass the first initiation under the Second Ray and those who do not pass it. They must then continue in their abuse of power, seeking to elevate one worded expression as the absolute and superior truth that all people on earth respect and follow and worship. Right there is the first challenge under the initiations of the Second Ray. When you have gone through the initiations of the First Ray, you are ready to pass this challenge at inner levels. Many of the people who read this will already have passed the initiation at inner levels. The big question is: "Has your outer mind tuned in to your inner progress?"

Have you with the outer, conscious mind recognized that any worded expression is just one possible way to describe the reality that is beyond words? It is not the *only* truth. It is not the only possible expression, and therefore, it must not be turned into a closed mental box. If you close your mental box, then I, Lanto, cannot teach you. You must then go back and learn from the School of Hard Knocks where you get into conflicts with other people and continue these conflicts for as many embodiments as it takes before you are ready to consider that perhaps a particular worded expression, as good as it might be, is only one possible way to describe that which truly cannot be described in words.

Not even the Word of God can capture the fullness of God. Not even the word of Lanto can capture the fullness of the spirit that I AM. If you think you can know me through words, you have not even started to know me. If you use the words that I give as a way to attune the radio of your mind to my Presence, then I will impart to you my Presence. Then, you will pass the initiation of shedding the first perception filter on the Second Ray of Wisdom.

Lanto I AM. I AM a spirit. I AM *more* than what could ever be described in words, and I long to impart to you that more. Before I *can,* you must be willing to let go of any worded expression that you think describes me, or describes God, or describes the spiritual reality, or describes life on earth. Use these words that I have given you to start opening your mind to an experience that is entirely beyond words. Lanto I AM. "Lanto" is just a word. "I" is just a word. "AM" is just a word. I AM *more.* Know me as that *more* and you shall know yourself as the *more*.

5 | I INVOKE THE SPIRIT OF LANTO

In the name I AM THAT I AM, Jesus Christ, I call to my I AM Presence to flow through the I Will Be Presence that I AM and give this invocation with full power. I call to beloved Elohim Apollo and Lumina and Hercules and Amazonia, Archangel Jophiel and Christine and Michael and Faith, Master Lanto and Master MORE to help me overcome all tendency to use wisdom as a form of competition or a weapon against others. Help me see and surrender all patterns that block my oneness with Master Lanto and my oneness with my I AM Presence, including …

[Make personal calls]

1. I submit myself to my teacher

1. Beloved Lanto, I submit myself to you as my teacher. I am willing to have you awaken me so I can see the Buddha Nature in myself, the Buddha Nature in everything that surrounds me, and the Buddha Nature in *you* so that I will know that we are indeed equals, as all self-aware beings are equals in the reality of the light of the Wisdom of God.

> Beloved Apollo, with your second ray,
> you open my eyes to see a new day,
> I see through duality's lies and deceit,
> transcending the mindset producing defeat.
>
> **Beloved Apollo, thou Elohim Gold,**
> **your radiant light my eyes now behold,**
> **as pages of wisdom you gently unfold,**
> **I feel I am free from all that is old.**

2. Ultimate wisdom is that all life is one, that all is the Buddha Nature, and thus, differentiation in form does not mean differentiation in value.

> Beloved Apollo, in your flame I know,
> that your living wisdom is always a flow,
> in your light I see my own highest will,
> immersed in the stream that never stands still.
>
> **Beloved Apollo, your light makes it clear,**
> **why we have taken embodiment here,**
> **working to raise our own cosmic sphere,**
> **together we form the tip of the spear.**

5 | I Invoke the Spirit of Lanto

3. Value is a wholly artificial concept created by the mind that has separated itself from the reality of wisdom, that has created the illusion that it is separated from the Buddha Nature, that the Buddha Nature is not where it is, that the separate mind has created a separate abode that has somehow shut out the Buddha Nature.

> Beloved Apollo, exposing all lies,
> I hereby surrender all ego-based ties,
> I know my perception is truly the key,
> to transcending the serpentine duality.
>
> **Beloved Apollo, we heed now your call,**
> **drawing us into Wisdom's Great Hall,**
> **exposing all lies causing the fall,**
> **you help us reclaim the oneness of all.**

4. Beloved Lanto, I am willing to penetrate the veils of anti-wisdom, the veils created by the separate mind, the dualistic mind, the serpentine mind, the fallen mind.

> Beloved Apollo, your wisdom so clear,
> in oneness with you, no serpent I fear,
> the beam in my eye I'm willing to see,
> I'm free from the serpent's own duality.
>
> **Beloved Apollo, my eyes now I raise,**
> **I see that the Earth is in a new phase,**
> **I willingly stand in your piercing gaze,**
> **empowered, I exit duality's maze.**

5. Beloved Lanto, I am willing for you go in and look at me, look at my state of mind, look at my particular perception filter, look at the core beliefs that make up my perception filter, and then address those beliefs.

> O Hercules Blue, you fill every space,
> with infinite Power and infinite Grace,
> you embody the key to creativity,
> the will to transcend into Infinity.

> **O Hercules Blue, in oneness with thee,**
> **I open my heart to your reality,**
> **in feeling your flame, so clearly I see,**
> **transcending my self is the true alchemy.**

6. I understand that, when I am at a certain level of consciousness, I cannot instantly shed all of the perception filters through which I am looking at life.

> O Hercules Blue, I lovingly raise,
> my voice in giving God infinite praise,
> I'm grateful for playing my personal part,
> In God's infinitely intricate work of art.

> **O Hercules Blue, all life now you heal,**
> **enveloping all in your Blue-flame Seal,**
> **your electric-blue fire within us reveal,**
> **our innermost longing for all that is real.**

7. Beloved Lanto, I am willing to be patient with myself and follow your gradual instructions. I realize that the spiritual path has certain stages. What will get me through one stage, will not get me through the next stage.

O Hercules Blue, I pledge now my life,
in helping this planet transcend human strife,
duality's lies are pierced by your light,
restoring the fullness of my inner sight.

O Hercules Blue, I'm one with your will,
all space in my being with Blue Flame you fill,
your power allows me to forge on until,
I pierce every veil and climb every hill.

8. I cannot power my way through the initiations of the Second Ray. I surrender the dream that I need to study until I find this secret book, this secret insight, the secret wisdom, that will now propel me to the mastery of the Second Ray.

O Hercules Blue, your Temple of Light,
revealed to us all through our inner sight,
a beacon that radiates light to the Earth,
bringing about our planet's rebirth.

O Hercules Blue, all life you defend,
giving us power to always transcend,
in you the expansion of self has no end,
as I in God's infinite spirals ascend.

9. Beloved Lanto, I realize there is a large difference between my state of consciousness and your ascended mind. I will not be discouraged by this. I will acknowledge that in order for me to tune in to your mind, I need to look beyond my current perception filter.

Accelerate my Awakeness, I AM real,
Accelerate my Awakeness, all life heal,
Accelerate my Awakeness, I AM MORE,
Accelerate my Awakeness, all will soar.

Accelerate my Awakeness! (3X)
Beloved Apollo and Lumina.
Accelerate my Awakeness! (3X)
Beloved Jophiel and Christine.
Accelerate my Awakeness! (3X)
Beloved Master Lanto.
Accelerate my Awakeness! (3X)
Beloved I AM.

2. I will attune to the initiations of the Second Ray

1. Beloved Lanto, I realize that you communicate in a way that is holistic and all-encompassing. You are not just communicating through ideas, but through feelings, sensations, experiences.

Jophiel Archangel, in wisdom's great light,
all serpentine lies exposed to my sight.
So subtle the lies that creep through the mind,
yet you are the greatest teacher I find.

Jophiel Archangel, exposing all lies,
Jophiel Archangel, cutting all ties.
Jophiel Archangel, clearing the skies,
Jophiel Archangel, my mind truly flies.

5 | I Invoke the Spirit of Lanto

2. Beloved Lanto, I know that what you are seeking to communicate to me is not the words or the meaning that the linear mind attaches to those words. I want to experience the holistic communication that you are projecting from your level of consciousness towards mine.

> Jophiel Archangel, your wisdom I hail,
> your sword cutting through duality's veil.
> As you show the way, I know what is real,
> from serpentine doubt, I instantly heal.
>
> **Jophiel Archangel, exposing all lies,**
> **Jophiel Archangel, cutting all ties.**
> **Jophiel Archangel, clearing the skies,**
> **Jophiel Archangel, my mind truly flies.**

3. Beloved Lanto, I want the inner, mystical, holistic experience that will transform my consciousness. I will seek to go beyond the words so that I may experience the all-encompassing holistic nature of your communication.

> Jophiel Archangel, your reality,
> the best antidote to duality.
> No lie can remain in your Presence so clear,
> with you on my side, no serpent I fear.
>
> **Jophiel Archangel, exposing all lies,**
> **Jophiel Archangel, cutting all ties.**
> **Jophiel Archangel, clearing the skies,**
> **Jophiel Archangel, my mind truly flies.**

4. Beloved Lanto, I want to grasp enough of the qualities of the Second Ray with my outer mind so that I am able to tune in to that ray. When my mind leaves the body during sleep, I want to travel to your Royal Teton Retreat.

> Jophiel Archangel, God's mind is in me,
> and through your clear light, its wisdom I see.
> Divisions all vanish, as I see the One,
> and truly, the wholeness of mind I have won.

> **Jophiel Archangel, exposing all lies,**
> **Jophiel Archangel, cutting all ties.**
> **Jophiel Archangel, clearing the skies,**
> **Jophiel Archangel, my mind truly flies.**

5. Beloved Lanto, I see that your task is to help me go beyond my perception filter. I know that I come with a perception filter, and I will not expect that you will validate my perception of life. I am ready to let go of that perception filter.

> Michael Archangel, in your flame so blue,
> there is no more night, there is only you.
> In oneness with you, I am filled with your light,
> what glorious wonder, revealed to my sight.

> **Michael Archangel, your Faith is so strong,**
> **Michael Archangel, oh sweep me along.**
> **Michael Archangel, I'm singing your song,**
> **Michael Archangel, with you I belong.**

6. Beloved Lanto, I want to make the shift into the initiations of the Second Ray. I surrender the drive to power my way through wisdom, through the initiations of the Second Ray.

Michael Archangel, protection you give,
within your blue shield, I ever shall live.
Sealed from all creatures, roaming the night,
I remain in your sphere, of electric blue light.

Michael Archangel, your Faith is so strong,
Michael Archangel, oh sweep me along.
Michael Archangel, I'm singing your song,
Michael Archangel, with you I belong.

7. I realize that it is not enough to just study and fill my mind and program my mind with all this wisdom in order to pass the exam. God Wisdom is not worldly wisdom.

Michael Archangel, what power you bring,
as millions of angels, praises will sing.
Consuming the demons, of doubt and of fear,
I know that your Presence, will always be near.

Michael Archangel, your Faith is so strong,
Michael Archangel, oh sweep me along.
Michael Archangel, I'm singing your song,
Michael Archangel, with you I belong.

8. I want to engage the initiations of Divine Wisdom, and I surrender my image of worldly wisdom. I surrender the perception filter of thinking that wisdom should be used as a weapon.

Michael Archangel, God's will is your love,
you bring to us all, God's light from Above
God's will is to see, all life taking flight,
transcendence of self, our most sacred right.

**Michael Archangel, your Faith is so strong,
Michael Archangel, oh sweep me along.
Michael Archangel, I'm singing your song,
Michael Archangel, with you I belong.**

9. I surrender the tendency to use the power I gained during the initiations of the First Ray to reinforce this perception filter. I surrender the desire to study so hard that I become better, wiser, smarter, more knowledgeable than other students.

With angels I soar,
as I reach for MORE.
The angels so real,
their love all will heal.
The angels bring peace,
all conflicts will cease.
With angels of light,
we soar to new height.

**The rustling sound of angel wings,
what joy as even matter sings,
what joy as every atom rings,
in harmony with angel wings.**

3. I am free of using wisdom against others

1. I surrender all desire to debate as the intellectuals and turn it into a competition to see who can outsmart and outmaneuver others. I surrender the tendency to think there *must* be an opposition, there must be something that is *true* and something that is *false*.

5 | I Invoke the Spirit of Lanto

Master Lanto, golden wise,
expose in me the ego's lies.
Master Lanto, will to be,
I will to win my mastery.

**O Holy Spirit, flow through me,
I am the open door for thee.
O mighty rushing stream of Light,
transcendence is my sacred right.**

2. I surrender the consciousness that those who know what is true must overpower those who do not have the same way of looking at life, and therefore must be wrong, false, of the devil.

Master Lanto, balance all,
for wisdom's balance I do call.
Master Lanto, help me see,
that balance is the Golden key.

**O Holy Spirit, flow through me,
I am the open door for thee.
O mighty rushing stream of Light,
transcendence is my sacred right.**

3. I surrender the belief that my spiritual knowledge, whether it comes from the ascended masters or some other teaching or teacher, is superior to all others. I know ultimate wisdom is beyond words. It is holistic, it is all-encompassing, it is an experience.

Master Lanto, from Above,
I call forth discerning love.
Master Lanto, love's not blind,
through love, God vision I will find.

> O Holy Spirit, flow through me,
> I am the open door for thee.
> O mighty rushing stream of Light,
> transcendence is my sacred right.

4. I know that in the translation into words, the all-encompassing, holistic nature is somewhat lost. The words are only tools for transcendence.

> Master Lanto, pure I am,
> intentions pure as Christic lamb.
> Master Lanto, I will transcend,
> acceleration now my truest friend.

> **O Holy Spirit, flow through me,**
> **I am the open door for thee.**
> **O mighty rushing stream of Light,**
> **transcendence is my sacred right.**

5. I see that when I take a worded expression and turn it into an absolute truth, then I have lost Divine Wisdom. I have gained worldly or human wisdom, but that is a poor substitute for the real thing.

> Master Lanto, I am whole,
> no more division in my soul.
> Master Lanto, healing flame,
> all balance in your sacred name.

> **O Holy Spirit, flow through me,**
> **I am the open door for thee.**
> **O mighty rushing stream of Light,**
> **transcendence is my sacred right.**

6. I surrender the pattern of abusing wisdom with power. I surrender the desire to elevate one expression with words as a superior form of wisdom and project it upon everything, thinking it must conform to this wisdom.

> Master Lanto, serve all life,
> as I transcend all inner strife.
> Master Lanto, peace you give,
> to all who want to truly live.

> **O Holy Spirit, flow through me,**
> **I am the open door for thee.**
> **O mighty rushing stream of Light,**
> **transcendence is my sacred right.**

7. I surrender the tendency to project on the Living Buddha and the Living Christ that he or she must conform to my perception filter. The Living Buddha and the Living Christ have come to help me escape my mental box and I am willing to be free.

> Master Lanto, free to be,
> in balanced creativity.
> Master Lanto, we employ,
> your balance as the key to joy.

> **O Holy Spirit, flow through me,**
> **I am the open door for thee.**
> **O mighty rushing stream of Light,**
> **transcendence is my sacred right.**

8. I see that my mental box is closed because I have taken one statement of wisdom and I have applied power to elevate it to the status of being absolute. My statement of wisdom may be perfectly valid, but it is not the *only* way to describe reality. It is not the *only truth*, for there is no one and only truth.

> Master Lanto, balance all,
> the seven rays upon my call.
> Master Lanto, I take flight,
> my threefold flame a blazing light.

> **O Holy Spirit, flow through me,**
> **I am the open door for thee.**
> **O mighty rushing stream of Light,**
> **transcendence is my sacred right.**

9. Any worded expression is just one description. There is more than one that is valid and useful, but they are all only descriptions and I want oneness with the spirit behind them.

> Lanto dear, your Presence here,
> filling up my inner sphere.
> Life is now a sacred flow,
> God Wisdom I on all bestow.

> **O Holy Spirit, flow through me,**
> **I am the open door for thee.**
> **O mighty rushing stream of Light,**
> **transcendence is my sacred right.**

4. I reach for the Spirit of Wisdom

1. Descriptions can be useful for transcending the words and gaining the holistic experience of the Spirit of Wisdom, the spirit that is the originator of the Word but that is more than the words, that is more than the form.

> Master MORE, come to the fore,
> I will absorb your flame of MORE.
> Master MORE, my will so strong,
> my power center cleared by song.

> **O Holy Spirit, flow through me,**
> **I am the open door for thee.**
> **O mighty rushing stream of Light,**
> **transcendence is my sacred right.**

2. I hereby do, with my outer, conscious mind, recognize that any worded expression is just one possible way to describe the reality that is beyond words.

> Master MORE, your wisdom flows,
> as my attunement ever grows.
> Master MORE, we have a tie,
> that helps me see through Serpent's lie.

> **O Holy Spirit, flow through me,**
> **I am the open door for thee.**
> **O mighty rushing stream of Light,**
> **transcendence is my sacred right.**

3. A description is not the *only* truth, it is not the only possible expression. I surrender the desire to turn a teaching into a closed mental box. I am being taught directly by Master Lanto.

> Master MORE, your love so pink,
> there is no purer love, I think.
> Master MORE, you set me free,
> from all conditionality.

**O Holy Spirit, flow through me,
I am the open door for thee.
O mighty rushing stream of Light,
transcendence is my sacred right.**

4. Not even the word of Lanto can capture the fullness of the spirit that he is. Beloved Lanto, I want to know you beyond words.

> Master MORE, I will endure,
> your discipline that makes me pure.
> Master MORE, intentions true,
> as I am always one with you.

**O Holy Spirit, flow through me,
I am the open door for thee.
O mighty rushing stream of Light,
transcendence is my sacred right.**

5. I use the outer word as a way to attune the radio of my mind to Lanto's Presence, and I know Lanto will impart to me his Presence.

Master MORE, my vision raised,
the will of God is always praised.
Master MORE, creative will,
raising all life higher still.

**O Holy Spirit, flow through me,
I am the open door for thee.
O mighty rushing stream of Light,
transcendence is my sacred right.**

6. I am passing the initiation of shedding the first perception filter on the Second Ray of Wisdom by recognizing that Lanto is a spirit.

Master MORE, your peace is power,
the demons of war it will devour.
Master MORE, we serve all life,
our flames consuming war and strife.

**O Holy Spirit, flow through me,
I am the open door for thee.
O mighty rushing stream of Light,
transcendence is my sacred right.**

7. Beloved Lanto, I know you are *more* than what could ever be described in words, and I am receiving and absorbing that more.

Master MORE, I am so free,
eternal bond from you to me.
Master MORE, I find rebirth,
in flow of your eternal mirth.

**O Holy Spirit, flow through me,
I am the open door for thee.
O mighty rushing stream of Light,
transcendence is my sacred right.**

8. Beloved Lanto, I am willing to let go of any worded expression that describes you, or describes God, or describes the spiritual reality, or describes life on earth.

Master MORE, you balance all,
the seven rays upon my call.
Master MORE, forever MORE,
I am the Spirit's open door.

**O Holy Spirit, flow through me,
I am the open door for thee.
O mighty rushing stream of Light,
transcendence is my sacred right.**

9. Beloved Lanto, I am opening my mind to an experience that is entirely beyond words. I know you are more and I know you as that *more*. I know myself as the *more*.

Master MORE, your Presence here,
filling up my inner sphere.
Life is now a sacred flow,
God Power I on all bestow.

**O Holy Spirit, flow through me,
I am the open door for thee.
O mighty rushing stream of Light,
transcendence is my sacred right.**

Sealing:

In the name of the Divine Mother, I fully accept that the power of these calls is used to set free the Ma-ter light, so it can outpicture the perfect vision of Christ for my own life, for all people and for the planet. In the name I AM THAT I AM, it is done! Amen.

6 | WISDOM AND ILLUMINATION

I AM the ascended master Lord Lanto, and I come to give you the keys to understanding the initiations you go through at the second level after you start the process of being initiated on the retreat of the Second Ray. The first level is the level of using wisdom through the First Ray of power, and, naturally, the second level is that of using wisdom through the Second Ray of wisdom. This is then a double dose of wisdom. The initiation that you go through at this level is that you need to learn more about how wisdom can be used and misused.

Wisdom is not a competition

I have told you how we put people in groups and let them stay there until they are done using wisdom to overpower each other. At the next level, we again put people in groups, and now we have them take a particular issue, and then we have them come up with arguments for or against the issue. Again, it is somewhat amazing how eager many students are to show how wise they are, how good they are at arguing their case. You have been so programmed on earth to think that life is some kind of competition. If you are being initiated in the Second Ray of wisdom there must be a competition on who knows the most, who has the best argument, the most convincing argument. Yet, at the retreat of the Royal Teton, we have a different purpose. We are not seeking to teach our students how to come up with the best argument on earth. We are seeking to help them transcend the very state of consciousness that believes there is an ultimate argument.

Think how you have been programmed by the institutions of this world, especially the religious and the educational institutions. You have been programmed to think that somewhere there exists this ultimate wisdom, this ultimate standard, against which everything else must be measured. Anything that is not in accordance with this ultimate wisdom is false and should be judged.

The people who espouse this false wisdom should be judged likewise, according to whatever belief system they have chosen to accept. If, for example, you are a Christian, then you will say that those who do not agree with your version of wisdom surely must be the anti-Christ. They must be of the devil and they must deserve to go to hell. God wants them to go to hell. God at least wants them to get off the earth, and maybe God needs your help in killing these people so that they can get off the earth.

How many times in history have you seen this pattern repeat itself? How many places in the world do you see it right now where there are people who believe that they have a superior form of wisdom that entitles them, obligates them, to kill their fellow men? How many places in the West, where you are not seeing so many people willing to kill, do you still see people in the academic world who are willing to argue and argue and argue, seeking to literally psychologically destroy those who do not accept their wisdom as superior?

The second initiation on the Second Ray

What we do in our groups in the Royal Teton Retreat is that we let people argue until they get tired of it, until they have had enough of the argument. We watch our groups. We see when people on an individual basis begin to fall more and more silent. Instead of being eager to put forth their wisdom, they now fall silent. They sit there; they listen; they watch. We can tell that now their minds are beginning to be open. They are beginning to wonder how it can be that you seemingly cannot resolve a debate, a controversy. How is it that no matter how good of an argument that you construct, it is always possible to construct a counter-argument? How is it that people can become so attached to a particular argument that they will not see anything else? Is there, perhaps, something else to see beyond these arguments?

Ah, yes my beloved, this is when students begin to be open to the next level of initiation. What we then do is we take them aside. We leave those who are still willing to argue in their groups where they can argue, and they have new people, new lifestreams, coming in that they can argue with, and this can go on until they, too, tire of it. We take those who have begun to open their minds and we take them to a special classroom where we have the ability to use a large screen to display what happens at an energy level. We can actually show these lifestreams what happens in their energy fields as they engage in these arguments. We are able to visually illustrate how the light flows from your I AM Presence into your four lower bodies. We are then able to show also how we from the ascended realm can release a particular impulse of wisdom into the mind of an individual student.

We can show graphically, visually, what that impulse looks like and how it is made up of something that might be compared to the ideal forms taught by the philosopher Plato.

These are basic geometric shapes, not as simple as triangles and squares and circles, but more complex geometric shapes. When you see them visually, you see their beauty, their harmony, their balance, and you see how these geometric shapes can interact with any other geometric shape at this pure level without destroying it, without canceling it out, without creating a negative interference pattern. We can now show graphically what happens as this impulse of wisdom made up by these pure geometric shapes descends into the identity body of a particular student. We can make visual exactly what happens as the pure impulse of wisdom begins to interact with the geometric shapes in the student's identity body. These shapes will, of course, be determined by the level of consciousness of the student. Because that level, by the nature of the student undergoing this initiation, is not so high, it is obvious that there will be an interference between the geometric forms in the student's identity body and the forms of the pure impulse of wisdom.

This means that, already in the identity body, the original pure pulse of wisdom is partially blocked, partially distorted. What descends into the student's mental body is barely recognizable compared to the original purity. We then show how what comes out of the identity body enters the mental body and begins to interact with the geometric forms stored there. Again, there is blockage, there is interference, there is distortion. We can now make visible what leaves the mental and enters the emotional body. Again, the impulse is diluted and changed and what finally enters the person's conscious mind is so diluted that it has virtually nothing to do with the original pure impulse.

When students first see this, they are always shocked. They are shocked at their inability to transfer a pure impulse of wisdom through their four lower bodies and have their conscious minds grasp at least some aspect of the pure impulse. Our aim is not to shock the students. The shock is simply an inevitable fact of seeing how much your own mind actually distorts what comes from your I AM Presence and the ascended realm. At this level of the path, the distortion is extensive, and the shock factor is, likewise, quite dramatic.

We, of course, help the students deal with this sense of shock because we make it very clear to them that this is perfectly natural, that they are in no way standing out from the rest of humanity in a negative manner. They are in fact standing out in a positive manner because they are more open than the majority of human beings on earth. They are more open to having their mental box challenged and expanded.

How your role distorts wisdom

Our real aim with this exercise is to show people why there is no superior wisdom on earth. This begins by showing students that, in their identity bodies, they have adopted a certain state of identity. We have before talked about the process of taking embodiment by comparing it to the process of going into a theatre and putting on the costume and makeup associated with a particular role in a theatre performance. This is what happens at the identity level. Sometime in the past, in many cases in the distant past, you looked at the current conditions on earth, as imperfect as they were, and you decided to take on a particular role, a particular sense of identity. The role that you have taken on personally is quite complex, but in order to illustrate the point that I want to get across here, let me make it relatively simple.

Let us say that, in medieval times, you decided to take on the role of a Christian crusader. For whatever reasons, you decided that you wanted the experience of what it was like to be a Christian crusader going to the Holy Land and fighting to recapture

Jerusalem from the Muslims. When you take on this particular costume in your identity body, there are certain aspects of this role that are set in stone, that are taken for granted, that are beyond questioning. What defines the role of a Christian crusader is that you do not question the basic doctrines and outlook on life presented by the Catholic Church. This is simply beyond questioning.

When you, as a Conscious You, are outside of your role, you may be able to see that the Catholic Church presents only one possible view of reality, that it is not the ultimate wisdom and that it could be questioned in various ways. Once you step into the costume, the role of a Christian crusader, you are simply not able to see this, anymore than you are able to see the sky being blue if you are wearing yellow glasses. The glasses change what you physically see. The role you take on in the identity body also changes the way you look at life. You cannot see anything else.

You can of course, as a Conscious You, reconnect to the fact that you are pure awareness and temporarily step outside the role and experience that there is more to reality than what you see from inside the role. But if you do not do this, then you will literally experience life through the perception filter of that role. Whatever impulses come from the ascended realm through your I AM Presence will be completely distorted by the geometric forms that define the role. Before any impulse from your I AM Presence reaches your conscious mind, it will be distorted by the role, and therefore your conscious mind will experience that the impulse actually confirms and validates the worldview that you have through the perception filter of that role.

Once students begin to see this, it becomes relatively easy for them to see why there is no final argument and why you so often cannot reason with other people, why you cannot convince them that you are right and that their wisdom is wrong. Take the situation of the Crusades again. On one side you have Christian crusaders and on the other side you have the Muslims who are also on a crusade to establish their religion as the superior one. In the spiritual realm, there are no Christian lifestreams; there are no Muslim lifestreams. There is no Being in the ascended realm that identifies itself as a Christian or a Muslim. Being a Christian, being a Muslim is a role that is defined on earth, and it begins in the identity realm. It is not something you *are*. It is a role you step into and once you step into it, you see the world through the perception filter of the role.

A perception filter discards information

What does a filter do, my beloved? Let us say you have a water filter on the tap in your kitchen that filters your drinking water. What does that filter do? Well, it filters out certain things and it allows others to pass through. That is the very nature and function of a filter. Likewise, when you have a role in the identity body that you step into, you have a perception filter that filters out certain things and lets other things through. What we show students at this level is that the very nature of a perception filter is that it filters out anything that contradicts the role itself.

If you have stepped into the role of a Christian crusader, your perception filter will filter out any impulse, any knowledge, any wisdom, any insight that contradicts your Christian Medieval Catholic worldview. Someone else in physical embodiment can of course present you with an argument, for example, that Christianity is not the only true religion but that Islam is true because the prophet Mohammed had such and such authority from God. You will be able to hear this argument with your conscious mind, but your ability to consider the argument is completely determined by your perception filter. You will not be able to consider this argument neutrally or objectively if you have entered the role of a Christian crusader. You have taken on a perception filter, and it does not filter out things so that you cannot hear the argument, but it does filter out any sense that this argument could be valid. You are not even able to see any validity to the argument because any kind of validity and realism to an argument is filtered out by your perception filter. You can only see its flaws. You can only see it as false.

The futility of arguments

When we make visible on a screen what happens at the energy level when a Christian crusader confronts a Muslim crusader in argument, it is relatively easy for students to see that both sides are engaging in a completely futile attempt to convince and convert the other. We can make visible how the Christian crusader presents an argument for Christianity. We can show how the light from that person's I AM Presence is filtered through the geometric shapes in the persons identity body, and this gives a sense of realism and validity to the very worldview that makes up those geometric shapes at the identity level. We can then show how, when the Muslim crusader presents an argument, even though the person hears the words with the conscious mind, we can show how the energy impulse is actually filtered through both the emotional, mental, and identity levels. What actually comes to the conscious mind is the sense that the other persons argument is completely invalid because the sense of validity has been filtered out by the person's perception filter.

There is no possibility that the one person could convince the other when they are both at this level of consciousness and have no connection, no experience, of pure awareness. This is very easy for students to see. It is, therefore, very easy for them to also take a look at their own lives and look at how often they have engaged in arguments with other people. This is, in many cases, not necessarily philosophical arguments about the validity of this or that thought system. It can be arguments with spouses and children and parents where you engage in arguments about everyday matters or about your relationships. Again, we can show how the one person's perception filter makes that person believe that he or she is absolutely right and also filters out any sense of validity to the other person's argument.

We can show how there really is no outcome that could come out of these kind of arguments and discussions. It is simply a futile use of your energy, your time, and your attention. It is argument for arguments sake, and it comes from the ego's desire for some ultimate sense of security by being validated by other people. The ego is desperately seeking to get you to engage in these kind of arguments and to keep them running because that is how the ego and the spirits in your own consciousness are fed by the energy coming from your I AM Presence being distorted and directed into these futile arguments.

This is a difficult initiation for most students because they can clearly see how much energy, time and attention they have wasted on arguments that really had no chance of ever producing a constructive outcome. There is always a sense of regret and remorse because students realize that you only have a finite amount of time, energy, and attention when you are in physical embodiment. Why, then, use it on something that is futile?

How an argument can have potential benefits

After this inevitable moment of truth and sense of regret, we show students that, actually, the arguments have not been completely futile. Taking embodiment on earth in the present conditions means that you take on a certain role, a certain costume. You are meant to play that role, to outplay that role, until you have had enough of that experience and want something more. An inevitable part of the roles that are currently defined on earth is, in most cases, that it puts you in conflict with other people. You need to go through a certain amount of argumentation with others before you have had enough of that experience and can begin to question your role. From a larger perspective, the arguments were not completely wasted because they brought you closer and closer to that saturation point where you are now open to a different approach. You are now open to questioning your approach, questioning your role, questioning your perception filter.

Is this really the only way to look at life? Is it really the only way to live that I am constantly arguing with other people? Is the argumentation possibly a function of the way I look at life? If I am tired of arguing with other people, is it possible that the only way out of this state is that I begin to look at myself, that I begin to question my outlook on life, my perception filter?

Your role attracts people and experiences

We can also make visible on the screen a sort of map, like we have talked about before, where you can look at the earth and a satellite photo at night makes visible where there are light areas in and around the major cities. We can show how there are energy connections between people, and we can show students that they will attract people with the same level of consciousness, with the same kind of role.

If you have taken on a role that is defined in opposition to someone else, you will inevitably attract such people to your life. If you had taken on the role of Christian crusader, is it not obvious that this role is defined in opposition to a Muslim crusader? It really has no meaning if it does not have an opponent. Many of the roles that you have created today are far more complex, far more subtle. They still, in their very definition, incorporate some kind of opponent who opposes you so you can argue with them and engage in these banterings back and forth.

As long as this is the experience you desire to have, there is nothing wrong with this. When you have become saturated by that experience, then the only way out is to begin to question whether you really need to be playing that role forever or whether there is more to you than the role, and therefore you can begin to step outside the role and look at life differently.

The crusade to validate the ego

Students can then come to an important turning point on their path. They can begin to question whether they really, truly, want to continue their crusade to validate their egos. In many cases, this crusade to validate the ego has taken on a disguise as being altruistic, as serving some greater cause. We have, in other teachings, talked about the epic mindset. My beloved brother, Jesus, has given a profound book on ego dramas and how this epic mindset sets up dramas with other people [See *Freedom from Ego Dramas*]. We can show students how they, in many cases, use even a spiritual teaching, even an ascended master teaching, in this crusade to convince other people about the validity of the teaching. When you look deeper, you see that this is just a disguise, it is all camouflage for the ego's desire to validate itself.

It is necessary at this stage to show students how they can even use the teachings of the ascended masters in this crusade for ego validation. There is no student at this level who has not done this, who has not gone through this. It is perfectly natural that you go through this phase. When students are open to this level of initiation, we can show them that this is perfectly natural at their current level of the path. When you first find the teachings of the ascended masters, it is perfectly natural and perfectly in order that you become enthusiastic.

After all, our teachings do explain many things that are not explained by mainstream religion or by materialistic philosophies and therefore, you do increase your understanding. You come to see many things that you did not see before. You find answers to many questions. It is natural in the beginning that you become so enthusiastic that you think that if only all other people could come to understand what you understand, the world would be changed, certain problems would disappear, there would be greater peace and understanding among people.

It is important to understand that this feeling is not entirely wrong. If all people on earth embraced an ascended master teaching, there *would* be greater understanding, cooperation, and peace between people. There is no question about this; yet, what we aim to show students at this level is that, when you engage in these arguments that we have shown visually, even an ascended master teaching will not convince other people against their perception filters. An ascended master teaching is no more effective for convincing a Christian crusader than a Muslim teaching is because an ascended master teaching, even though it contains a higher degree of validity and wisdom than any other teaching currently found on earth, is still expressed in words.

This is what I talked about in my last discourse. Words are words. They must be interpreted, and when you interpret certain words through your perception filter, the perception filter will filter out the validity of those words that contradict your worldview. It does not matter whether those words come from the ascended realm or from the Bible or the Koran or from some scientific finding and report. Your perception filter will filter out the validity of any argument that contradicts the perception filter and the role that defined it.

How students go beyond their perception filters

It is absolutely wonderful for a teacher to see what happens when students finally get this, when they truly grasp this reality! You can see how a great burden is lifted from them. Instead of carrying this responsibility of having to change the world by converting other people, they can now begin to let go of this heavy yoke, truly put upon them by the fallen beings and the false teachers. Many students have come to believe that this yoke was put upon them by the ascended masters. They believe that we are the ones that want them to go out and convert everyone else to our teachings, that we want them to go out and do battle and show the falsity of other people's teachings and other ideas. When students finally realize and accept that this has never been our aim, then you can see how they suddenly stand up more straight. They feel lighter. They look back at their lives and they realize: "Oh, I never had to go through all that. It was not the masters who wanted me to go through all these arguments and conflicts. It was only the ego and the false teachers."

That is when they can begin to look at us differently. As I said in my previous discourse, you do not see me as I AM. When you realize that I am not the one who wants you to go out and battle other viewpoints and use the teachings of the ascended masters as a battering ram to break down the fortifications around the minds of other people, then you can begin to relate to me in a different way. It is almost as if students, for the first time, are able to look at me with an open mind. You can see how something clicks in their minds, and they have the thought: "Who is this Ascended Master Lanto, really?"

They realize that so far they have looked at me through a filter. They have thought that I was somehow forcing them to do something, wanting them to do something. Now, they are able to take off this filter and look at me with a more neutral awareness. That is, of course, the moment I am waiting for. As all ascended masters, it is natural for me to share my Presence. I am always joyful, happy, and grateful when I am able to share a more full expression of my Presence with a particular student or group of students.

Coming into oneness with the teacher

How do you pass the initiations of the Second Ray? Not by listening to me as if I am a teacher standing at the head of the class talking down to you. You pass the initiations of the Second Ray by coming into oneness with me. You cannot come into oneness with me as long as you think I am forcing you, that you have to do certain things because I am there as the strict teacher. Why would you want to come into oneness with a teacher who is like that? Why would you want to come into oneness with any teacher?

When students first come to my retreat, they actually do not come with an attitude where they are able to learn from me. They come with this need to overpower others with wisdom. Do you think this is restricted only to their fellow students? Nay, you will be amazed at how many students come to my retreat and want to engage me in an argument. They have a preconceived opinion of how I, as the Chohan of the Second Ray, should be, what the Second Ray is like, what the wisdom of the Second Ray is, what the ultimate wisdom is. They often engage in arguments to try to prove that to me. That is, they engage in one-sided arguments, for I do not engage them. I either remain silent, which often infuriates them, or I seek to neutralize their questions, their projections, with a certain question.

Teaching by asking questions

You may know that the ancient Greek philosopher Socrates was known for not really teaching but asking questions that helped people clarify their own views and question their preconceived opinions. Well, Socrates did not invent this method. It has long been used by masters of the Second Ray and, of course, all the rays, for there is always a perception filter to be questioned, is there not?

Then, of course, we have students on the second level (wisdom and illumination) who also like to argue with me at a certain level because they think that I am imposing some restriction upon them, something they have to live up to. They are eager to show me how wise they are, how good they are at using arguments, how good they are at twisting a certain idea or belief system to validate them and their egos.

This, of course, makes it impossible for me to teach them anything. *They* are trying to teach *me,* yet, of course, they have not yet ascended, have they? It is not likely that I can learn anything from them that I have not already gone through myself in the process of qualifying for my ascension. It takes time before a student sees that arguments are just arguments, words are just words, and they never lead to a decisive outcome. This can lead the student to the realization: "But I am just arguing. I am arguing with other people. I am even arguing with the teacher, but it never leads to a decisive outcome for me because it does not shift me to a higher level of consciousness. I am not taking the leap from my current level to the next level up. Actually, the more I argue, the more I solidify my current level of consciousness."

Ascended teachers don't want superiority

When students begin to realize this, then there is a shift and that is when they begin to look at me in a new way. They realize that: "Master Lanto is not really arguing with me. He's not really trying to convince me of anything. He's not asking me to prove my ego right, to prove my worldview right. What is he doing then? What kind of being is he?" That is when the students can begin to go beyond the traditional view coming from earth of what it means to a teacher. They think that I am supposed to stand there, at the head of the class, and talk down to them. I am going to give them some knowledge that they can take, memorize, and then recite back to me—and *that* will give them a good grade.

Teachers on earth are doing what? Well, most teachers on earth actually become teachers because they want to feel superior to the students. They are engaged in teaching in order to validate their egos. What they are teaching to the students – the ideas, the beliefs, the knowledge that they are teaching – is also a giant process of validating certain thought systems on earth. A teacher at the Catholic Seminary is seeking to validate the Catholic worldview. A teacher at a university is seeking to validate the materialistic worldview, in many cases. This is ego validation taken to a global scale, but it is still just that: ego validation. If you exclude enough contrary evidence, you can always prove your ego right, can you not?

This is what students begin to see, and when they begin to see it, they can realize that I am not that kind of a teacher! I have no need to validate myself. I have no need to validate a particular teaching expressed in words. I desire to take the student to the next level up so that the student does not engage in arguments for the purpose of validating the ego because the student locks in to the possibility of using wisdom in a higher way, a way that is based on love. There can be a love for other people, but there can also be a love for wisdom, not as a particular expression in words, but as an intricate combination of pure geometric forms.

So far, the student has only been able to see wisdom as expressed in words, but when the student begins to see the futility of arguing with words, then the student will, at some point, have at least a brief glimpse of the wisdom that is beyond words, the wisdom that is pure geometric shapes. When the student sees that, this is when you see their eyes light up. Oh, now, *now,* they have touched the hem of the master's garment! *Now* they have seen that there is more to Master Lanto than a teacher regurgitating words and predefined arguments and viewpoints.

I am a living teacher. I am not filled with words. I am filled with pure geometric shapes that bubble up from the innermost recesses of my Being like a spring where the water is bubbling up from the earth, the pure water, the life-giving water, the living waters of wisdom! This I AM. Master Lanto, I AM! Catch me if you can.

7 | I INVOKE ONENESS WITH LANTO

In the name I AM THAT I AM, Jesus Christ, I call to my I AM Presence to flow through the I Will Be Presence that I AM and give this invocation with full power. I call to beloved Elohim Apollo and Lumina, Archangel Jophiel and Christine, and Master Lanto to help me transcend all tendency to engage in arguments where I use wisdom as a weapon in a crusade to validate my ego. Help me see and surrender all patterns that block my oneness with Master Lanto and my oneness with my I AM Presence, including …

[Make personal calls]

1. I am clearing my four bodies from false wisdom

1. I am transcending the earthly programming that life is a competition. I see that being initiated in the Second Ray of wisdom is not a competition to show who knows the most, who has the best argument.

Beloved Apollo, with your second ray,
you open my eyes to see a new day,
I see through duality's lies and deceit,
transcending the mindset producing defeat.

Beloved Apollo, thou Elohim Gold,
your radiant light my eyes now behold,
as pages of wisdom you gently unfold,
I feel I am free from all that is old.

2. I am transcending the state of consciousness that believes there is an ultimate argument, there exists this ultimate wisdom, this ultimate standard, against which everything else must be measured.

Beloved Apollo, in your flame I know,
that your living wisdom is always a flow,
in your light I see my own highest will,
immersed in the stream that never stands still.

Beloved Apollo, your light makes it clear,
why we have taken embodiment here,
working to raise our own cosmic sphere,
together we form the tip of the spear.

3. I am transcending the state of consciousness that believes anything that is not in accordance with this ultimate wisdom is false and should be judged, and that the people believing it should be judged or forced to accept the superior wisdom.

Beloved Apollo, exposing all lies,
I hereby surrender all ego-based ties,
I know my perception is truly the key,
to transcending the serpentine duality.

> **Beloved Apollo, we heed now your call,**
> **drawing us into Wisdom's Great Hall,**
> **exposing all lies causing the fall,**
> **you help us reclaim the oneness of all.**

4. I am transcending the academic mindset that is willing to argue and argue, seeking to psychologically destroy those who do not accept one form of wisdom as superior.

> Beloved Apollo, your wisdom so clear,
> in oneness with you, no serpent I fear,
> the beam in my eye I'm willing to see,
> I'm free from the serpent's own duality.

> **Beloved Apollo, my eyes now I raise,**
> **I see that the Earth is in a new phase,**
> **I willingly stand in your piercing gaze,**
> **empowered, I exit duality's maze.**

5. I see that no matter how good of an argument I construct, it is always possible to construct a counter-argument. I am longing for a higher way to relate to other people, I am longing to grasp a higher form of wisdom.

> Beloved Apollo, with your second ray,
> you open my eyes to see a new day,
> I see through duality's lies and deceit,
> transcending the mindset producing defeat.

> **Beloved Apollo, thou Elohim Gold,**
> **your radiant light my eyes now behold,**
> **as pages of wisdom you gently unfold,**
> **I feel I am free from all that is old.**

6. I want to know and experience the pure wisdom, the ideal geometric shapes, that are being released by the masters of the second ray.

Beloved Apollo, in your flame I know,
that your living wisdom is always a flow,
in your light I see my own highest will,
immersed in the stream that never stands still.

**Beloved Apollo, your light makes it clear,
why we have taken embodiment here,
working to raise our own cosmic sphere,
together we form the tip of the spear.**

7. Master Lanto, help me clear my identity body of all false wisdom so that it does not block or distort the pure geometric wisdom released by you, but allows it to pass through to my mental body in a pure form.

Beloved Apollo, exposing all lies,
I hereby surrender all ego-based ties,
I know my perception is truly the key,
to transcending the serpentine duality.

**Beloved Apollo, we heed now your call,
drawing us into Wisdom's Great Hall,
exposing all lies causing the fall,
you help us reclaim the oneness of all.**

8. Master Lanto, help me clear my mental body of all false wisdom so that it does not block or distort the pure geometric wisdom released by you, but allows it to pass through to my emotional body in a pure form.

Beloved Apollo, your wisdom so clear,
in oneness with you, no serpent I fear,
the beam in my eye I'm willing to see,
I'm free from the serpent's own duality.

**Beloved Apollo, my eyes now I raise,
I see that the Earth is in a new phase,
I willingly stand in your piercing gaze,
empowered, I exit duality's maze.**

9. Master Lanto, help me clear my emotional body of all false wisdom so that it does not block or distort the pure geometric wisdom released by you, but allows it to pass through to my conscious mind in a pure form. I want to be able to transfer an impulse of wisdom through my four lower bodies and have my conscious mind grasp the pure impulse.

Accelerate my Awakeness, I AM real,
Accelerate my Awakeness, all life heal,
Accelerate my Awakeness, I AM MORE,
Accelerate my Awakeness, all will soar.

Accelerate my Awakeness! (3X)
Beloved Apollo and Lumina.
Accelerate my Awakeness! (3X)
Beloved Jophiel and Christine.
Accelerate my Awakeness! (3X)
Beloved Master Lanto.
Accelerate my Awakeness! (3X)
Beloved I AM.

2. I have had enough of arguments

1. Master Lanto, help me see how the role I have taken on at the identity level distorts the way I look at life and the way I look at wisdom.

> Jophiel Archangel, in wisdom's great light,
> all serpentine lies exposed to my sight.
> So subtle the lies that creep through the mind,
> yet you are the greatest teacher I find.
>
> **Jophiel Archangel, exposing all lies,**
> **Jophiel Archangel, cutting all ties.**
> **Jophiel Archangel, clearing the skies,**
> **Jophiel Archangel, my mind truly flies.**

2. Master Lanto, help my Conscious You reconnect to the fact that I am pure awareness. Help me temporarily step outside my role and experience that there is more to reality than what I see from inside the role.

> Jophiel Archangel, your wisdom I hail,
> your sword cutting through duality's veil.
> As you show the way, I know what is real,
> from serpentine doubt, I instantly heal.
>
> **Jophiel Archangel, exposing all lies,**
> **Jophiel Archangel, cutting all ties.**
> **Jophiel Archangel, clearing the skies,**
> **Jophiel Archangel, my mind truly flies.**

3. Master Lanto, help me see that before any impulse from my I AM Presence reaches my conscious mind, it will be distorted by my role. My conscious mind will experience that the impulse confirms and validates the worldview that I have through the perception filter of my role.

> Jophiel Archangel, your reality,
> the best antidote to duality.
> No lie can remain in your Presence so clear,
> with you on my side, no serpent I fear.

Jophiel Archangel, exposing all lies,
Jophiel Archangel, cutting all ties.
Jophiel Archangel, clearing the skies,
Jophiel Archangel, my mind truly flies.

4. I now see why there is no final argument and why I cannot reason with other people. The very nature of a perception filter is that it filters out anything that contradicts the role that defined the filter.

> Jophiel Archangel, God's mind is in me,
> and through your clear light, its wisdom I see.
> Divisions all vanish, as I see the One,
> and truly, the wholeness of mind I have won.

Jophiel Archangel, exposing all lies,
Jophiel Archangel, cutting all ties.
Jophiel Archangel, clearing the skies,
Jophiel Archangel, my mind truly flies.

5. Master Lanto, help me see how my own perception filter prevents me from considering an idea neutrally or objectively by filtering out any sense that this idea could be valid.

> Jophiel Archangel, in wisdom's great light,
> all serpentine lies exposed to my sight.
> So subtle the lies that creep through the mind,
> yet you are the greatest teacher I find.
>
> **Jophiel Archangel, exposing all lies,**
> **Jophiel Archangel, cutting all ties.**
> **Jophiel Archangel, clearing the skies,**
> **Jophiel Archangel, my mind truly flies.**

6. Master Lanto, help me take a look at my own life and see how often I have engaged in arguments with other people. Help me see that there really is no outcome that could come out of these kind of arguments and discussions. It is a futile use of energy, time and attention.

> Jophiel Archangel, your wisdom I hail,
> your sword cutting through duality's veil.
> As you show the way, I know what is real,
> from serpentine doubt, I instantly heal.
>
> **Jophiel Archangel, exposing all lies,**
> **Jophiel Archangel, cutting all ties.**
> **Jophiel Archangel, clearing the skies,**
> **Jophiel Archangel, my mind truly flies.**

7. Master Lanto, I vow that I will no longer engage in argument for arguments sake. I see that this tendency comes from the ego's desire for the ultimate sense of security by being validated by other people.

> Jophiel Archangel, your reality,
> the best antidote to duality.
> No lie can remain in your Presence so clear,
> with you on my side, no serpent I fear.

> **Jophiel Archangel, exposing all lies,**
> **Jophiel Archangel, cutting all ties.**
> **Jophiel Archangel, clearing the skies,**
> **Jophiel Archangel, my mind truly flies.**

8. Master Lanto, help me see how my ego is seeking to get me to engage in these kind of arguments and to keep them running. The ego and the spirits in my own consciousness are being fed as the energy from my I AM Presence is being distorted and directed into these futile arguments.

> Jophiel Archangel, God's mind is in me,
> and through your clear light, its wisdom I see.
> Divisions all vanish, as I see the One,
> and truly, the wholeness of mind I have won.

> **Jophiel Archangel, exposing all lies,**
> **Jophiel Archangel, cutting all ties.**
> **Jophiel Archangel, clearing the skies,**
> **Jophiel Archangel, my mind truly flies.**

9. Master Lanto, I hereby consciously decide that I have had enough of playing any role that puts me in constant conflict with other people. Help me see that the argumentation is a function of the way I look at life. I am willing to look at myself, to question my outlook on life, my perception filter.

With angels I soar,
as I reach for MORE.
The angels so real,
their love all will heal.
The angels bring peace,
all conflicts will cease.
With angels of light,
we soar to new height.

**The rustling sound of angel wings,
what joy as even matter sings,
what joy as every atom rings,
in harmony with angel wings.**

3. I transcend the need for ego validation

1. Master Lanto, help me see if I have taken on a role that is defined in opposition to someone else, causing me to attract such people to my life. I have had enough of this experience. Help me step outside my role and look at life differently.

Master Lanto, golden wise,
expose in me the ego's lies.
Master Lanto, will to be,
I will to win my mastery.

**O Holy Spirit, flow through me,
I am the open door for thee.
O mighty rushing stream of Light,
transcendence is my sacred right.**

2. I am at an important turning point on my path. Master Lanto, I am consciously deciding that I no longer want to continue my crusade to validate my ego.

> Master Lanto, balance all,
> for wisdom's balance I do call.
> Master Lanto, help me see,
> that balance is the Golden key.
>
> **O Holy Spirit, flow through me,**
> **I am the open door for thee.**
> **O mighty rushing stream of Light,**
> **transcendence is my sacred right.**

3. Master Lanto, help me see how this crusade to validate my ego has taken on a disguise as being altruistic, as serving some greater cause. Help me transcend the epic mindset that sets up dramas with other people.

> Master Lanto, from Above,
> I call forth discerning love.
> Master Lanto, love's not blind,
> through love, God vision I will find.
>
> **O Holy Spirit, flow through me,**
> **I am the open door for thee.**
> **O mighty rushing stream of Light,**
> **transcendence is my sacred right.**

4. Master Lanto, help me see how I have used the teachings of the ascended masters in this crusade for ego validation. I understand that this is a natural phase, but I have had enough of it.

> Master Lanto, pure I am,
> intentions pure as Christic lamb.
> Master Lanto, I will transcend,
> acceleration now my truest friend.

> O Holy Spirit, flow through me,
> I am the open door for thee.
> O mighty rushing stream of Light,
> transcendence is my sacred right.

5. In seeing and surrendering this crusade for ego validation, a great burden is lifted from me. Instead of carrying this responsibility of having to change the world by converting other people, I am letting go of this heavy yoke put upon me by the fallen beings and the false teachers.

> Master Lanto, I am whole,
> no more division in my soul.
> Master Lanto, healing flame,
> all balance in your sacred name.

> **O Holy Spirit, flow through me,**
> **I am the open door for thee.**
> **O mighty rushing stream of Light,**
> **transcendence is my sacred right.**

6. I now see that this yoke was *not* put upon me by the ascended masters. I see that I never had to go through all that. It was not the masters who wanted me to go through all these arguments and conflicts. It was only the ego and the false teachers.

> Master Lanto, serve all life,
> as I transcend all inner strife.
> Master Lanto, peace you give,
> to all who want to truly live.

> O Holy Spirit, flow through me,
> I am the open door for thee.
> O mighty rushing stream of Light,
> transcendence is my sacred right.

7. I now look at the ascended masters differently. Master Lanto, I want to see you as you are. I realize that you are not the one who wants me to go out and battle other viewpoints and use the teachings of the ascended masters as a battering ram to break down the fortifications around the minds of other people.

> Master Lanto, free to be,
> in balanced creativity.
> Master Lanto, we employ,
> your balance as the key to joy.

> O Holy Spirit, flow through me,
> I am the open door for thee.
> O mighty rushing stream of Light,
> transcendence is my sacred right.

8. Master Lanto, I want to relate to you in a different way. I want to look at you with an open mind. I see that I have so far looked at you through a filter. Help me take off this filter and look at you with neutral awareness.

> Master Lanto, balance all,
> the seven rays upon my call.
> Master Lanto, I take flight,
> my threefold flame a blazing light.

**O Holy Spirit, flow through me,
I am the open door for thee.
O mighty rushing stream of Light,
transcendence is my sacred right.**

9. Master Lanto, I want you to share your Presence with me. I want to experience the full expression of your Presence and absorb that Presence of Wisdom.

> Lanto dear, your Presence here,
> filling up my inner sphere.
> Life is now a sacred flow,
> God Wisdom I on all bestow.

**O Holy Spirit, flow through me,
I am the open door for thee.
O mighty rushing stream of Light,
transcendence is my sacred right.**

4. I am in oneness with Master Lanto

1. Master Lanto, help me see that you are not a traditional teacher talking down to me. Help me see that the key to passing the initiations of the Second Ray is to come into oneness with you.

> Master Lanto, golden wise,
> expose in me the ego's lies.
> Master Lanto, will to be,
> I will to win my mastery.

7 | I Invoke Oneness with Lanto

O Holy Spirit, flow through me,
I am the open door for thee.
O mighty rushing stream of Light,
transcendence is my sacred right.

2. Master Lanto, help me see and transcend my preconceived opinion of how you, as the Chohan of the Second Ray, should be, what the Second Ray is like, what the wisdom of the Second Ray is, what ultimate wisdom is.

Master Lanto, balance all,
for wisdom's balance I do call.
Master Lanto, help me see,
that balance is the Golden key.

O Holy Spirit, flow through me,
I am the open door for thee.
O mighty rushing stream of Light,
transcendence is my sacred right.

3. Master Lanto, help me see any tendency I have of wanting to engage you in argument, seeking to prove something to you. Help me transcend any desire to show you how wise I am, how good I am at using arguments, how good I am at twisting a certain idea or belief system to validate my ego.

Master Lanto, from Above,
I call forth discerning love.
Master Lanto, love's not blind,
through love, God vision I will find.

**O Holy Spirit, flow through me,
I am the open door for thee.
O mighty rushing stream of Light,
transcendence is my sacred right.**

4. Master Lanto, help me see how arguing with other people, even arguing with the teacher, never leads to a decisive outcome and does not shift me to a higher level of consciousness. The more I argue, the more I solidify my current level of consciousness. Help me take the leap from my current level to the next level up.

Master Lanto, pure I am,
intentions pure as Christic lamb.
Master Lanto, I will transcend,
acceleration now my truest friend.

**O Holy Spirit, flow through me,
I am the open door for thee.
O mighty rushing stream of Light,
transcendence is my sacred right.**

5. Master Lanto, I see that you are not arguing with me, you are not trying to convince me of anything. You are not asking me to prove my ego right, to prove my worldview right. I want to know what kind of Being you really are.

Master Lanto, I am whole,
no more division in my soul.
Master Lanto, healing flame,
all balance in your sacred name.

> O Holy Spirit, flow through me,
> I am the open door for thee.
> O mighty rushing stream of Light,
> transcendence is my sacred right.

6. Master Lanto, help me see rise to the next level up so that I do not engage in arguments for the purpose of validating the ego. Help me lock in to the possibility of using wisdom in a higher way, a way that is based on love.

> Master Lanto, serve all life,
> as I transcend all inner strife.
> Master Lanto, peace you give,
> to all who want to truly live.

> O Holy Spirit, flow through me,
> I am the open door for thee.
> O mighty rushing stream of Light,
> transcendence is my sacred right.

7. Master Lanto, help me see beyond the wisdom that is expressed in words. Help me experience the wisdom that is beyond words, the wisdom that is pure geometric shapes.

> Master Lanto, free to be,
> in balanced creativity.
> Master Lanto, we employ,
> your balance as the key to joy.

> O Holy Spirit, flow through me,
> I am the open door for thee.
> O mighty rushing stream of Light,
> transcendence is my sacred right.

8. Master Lanto, help me touch the hem of your garment! Help me see that there is more to Master Lanto than a teacher regurgitating words and predefined arguments and viewpoints.

> Master Lanto, balance all,
> the seven rays upon my call.
> Master Lanto, I take flight,
> my threefold flame a blazing light.
>
> **O Holy Spirit, flow through me,
> I am the open door for thee.
> O mighty rushing stream of Light,
> transcendence is my sacred right.**

9. Master Lanto, I AM experiencing you as a living teacher, filled with pure geometric shapes that bubble up from the innermost recesses of your Being, like a spring where the water is bubbling up from the earth, the pure water, the life-giving water, the living waters of wisdom! This is Master Lanto, and I AM one with this Presence of Wisdom.

> Lanto dear, your Presence here,
> filling up my inner sphere.
> Life is now a sacred flow,
> God Wisdom I on all bestow.
>
> **O Holy Spirit, flow through me,
> I am the open door for thee.
> O mighty rushing stream of Light,
> transcendence is my sacred right.**

Sealing:

In the name of the Divine Mother, I fully accept that the power of these calls is used to set free the Ma-ter light, so it can outpicture the perfect vision of Christ for my own life, for all people and for the planet. In the name I AM THAT I AM, it is done! Amen.

8 | WISDOM AND LOVE

I AM Lanto and I love you. Why else would I be here with planet earth if it were not for the fact that I love you? I love other lifestreams embodying on this planet. I love the planet itself, and I love the vision and the plan for this planet held in the minds of the ascended masters, in this age, the master Saint Germain.

I am an ascended being. Consider for a moment the vastness of the material universe. Consider how many stars, galaxies, and planets there are. They are innumerable. Now, consider that you had a spaceship that allowed you to freely roam anywhere in the material universe. Would you stay with this little planet, or would you go to far-away horizons to explore what is there? Well, I can assure you that the spiritual realm is far more vast and has far more interesting horizons to explore than does the material universe. When you ascend, this entire vastness of the spiritual realm is open to you. You can go almost anywhere that you are willing to apply yourself. Why then would an ascended master choose to stay with earth? It can be for only one reason: love.

You can validate any viewpoint

As I said in my last discourse on wisdom, what we aim to show students is that you can argue for or against any viewpoint. By excluding contrary evidence, you can prove any point you want to prove. You can validate any dualistic belief to the satisfaction of the ego and those who see through the perception filter of a particular role. There are people on earth who doubt the existence of ascended masters. There are people on earth who doubt our motives for being with earth. There are people who say we should have moved on rather than staying with earth.

These people are completely convinced that they are right, for they are looking at us through a particular perception filter. There are even many ascended master students who are sure that we are real, who are sure we have valid motives for remaining with earth, but who are, nevertheless, trying to force us to fit into a particular mental box. Again, if you pick and choose, you can find an ascended master teaching that validates almost anything you want to believe. Do you want to believe that the ascended masters are like individualized versions of the angry god in the sky, promoted by the three monotheistic religions for thousands of years? Well, if so, you can find certain teachings that seemingly validate this viewpoint, but we are much more than that view. We are much more than any view. What we aim to show people at the second stage of initiation in the Royal Teton Retreat is that, once you have created a closed mental box, it will filter out any contrary evidence; and thus, it becomes a closed system, a closed circle, a self-fulfilling prophecy.

Breaking free of the mental box—by love or by force

There is no way out of the mental box as long as you are looking at life through the perception filter that created the box in the first place. You cannot question the perception from inside the perception filter. You must use the Conscious You's ability to project itself outside of your current mental box and perception filter. What will propel the Conscious You to do this? In the School of Hard Knocks you can eventually come to a point where the knocks have become so hard, you are so beaten down by life, you are so frustrated, that you are willing to take a look outside your mental box in order to escape the pain.

At the Royal Teton Retreat, we have no intention of putting you through pain until the pain becomes so intense that you choose to seek an escape. We are not here to offer you an escape, and therefore, there comes that point at the third level of initiation where you cannot go any further until you develop a motivation that is based on love. You must love something more than your mental box. You must love a higher wisdom more than the wisdom defined by your perception filter.

If you do not have this love, you cannot move on. What we aim to do at the third level of initiation is to show students that you actually *do* have that love somewhere in your being. When you go deep enough, you realize that in your lifestream is a love for something that is beyond your current mental box. This love originated before you created your current mental box by stepping into your current role. It is the love that brought the Conscious You to take embodiment in the material universe. You have a love for seeing God's creation unfold. You have a love for your I AM Presence and your particular individualized God qualities. You have a love for expressing those God qualities, seeing that light radiating in the darkness of the material realm.

This is the motivation that we seek to help you rediscover. Certainly, you have to some degree already rediscovered this motivation as you went through the initiations on the First Ray, but we help you go deeper and reconnect to the love that brought you to this planet. We help you see how you can express love with greater wisdom, with greater discernment. At the Third Ray initiations at our retreat, we aim to help you see that when wisdom is expressed through love, something new suddenly dawns on you. You begin to realize that what people do with wisdom on earth is not driven by love, or rather, it is not driven by Divine Love; it is driven by human love. They use wisdom as the basis for judgment, including a value judgment that is so dear to the ego and the fallen beings, the false teachers.

Christ Discernment and human judgment

Wisdom becomes perverted through this false love, through this possessive, controlling love; and therefore, it is no longer Divine Wisdom. True Divine Wisdom gives you discernment, but discernment has nothing to do with human judgment. This is something that most students have never even thought of before. They have never considered that there could be a difference between Christ discernment and the judgment that springs from the mind of anti-Christ. From a superficial viewpoint, people are used to thinking that when you evaluate situations or people or ideas based on a sophisticated standard, then you are exercising discernment. Many people even think that this is Christ discernment.

Look at how many Christians are convinced that *their* church has the only true interpretation of the Bible, and its doctrines and worldview are surely based on what they would call Christ discernment, if they used that terminology. They are absolutely convinced that they are judging righteous judgment because they have the true interpretation of the words of Christ. In reality, what they have is a human interpretation of the words of Christ based on the mind of anti-Christ. They have imposed a false image upon the teachings of Christ, and they use this to judge other religions, all ideas, other interpretations of the Bible, and other people.

They judge other religions and those who have no religion, but they even judge their fellow Christians. In many of these small churches, especially in the United States, the members are convinced that they are special, even among all Christians. They are the ones who have the true teaching. They are the ones who are sure to go to heaven or are sure to recognize Jesus when he comes again in the second coming. When Jesus *does* come again, they are sure that they will be validated as the only ones who had the true teachings of Christ. This, of course, is not Christ discernment.

Unfortunately, there are even ascended master students who believe that they have Christ discernment, based on the teachings given by the ascended masters. Yet, as I have said, what we give are words. Words are open to interpretation, and what people do is that they interpret our words based on their existing perception filters. It is perfectly possible to take an ascended master teaching and use it to build a mental box that is fully as closed as the mental box of many fundamentalist Christian groups.

We have seen this happen in the last century or so where we have given our teachings publicly. We see it even today where there are groups of people who are convinced that they are the most advanced ascended master students on the planet, for they have taken a specific teaching, turned it into a closed mental box, and used it to judge the Living Word that we are still giving forth to those who are open to being messengers of the Living Word.

This is not Christ discernment, and this is what you need to see at the third level of initiation at the Royal Teton Retreat. Until you begin to literally experience the difference in vibration between Christ discernment and human judgment, you cannot move on. You cannot pass the initiations at the third level, the initiations of wisdom expressed through love.

Divine love does not restrict people's free will

Love does not judge. Divine Love does not judge, but human love is, indeed, entirely based on a judgment. Just look at how people in the world deal with the topic, the concept, of love. Look at how many people in their personal relationships seek to own or control the person that they say they love. They may think this is for that person's own good, but how is it for another person's good that you seek to force the free will of that person? Did God ever appoint you as the judge of how other people should exercise their free will?

We are sometimes having to be a little bit tough on students. We sometimes have to show them how they in their waking consciousness are exercising conditional love, possessive love, in their relationships with other people. We then show them a particular relationship and how they are dealing with a certain person, and we then ask them why they are doing this or that. They can always come up with an argument for why what they are doing is necessary for the other person's own good. We then sometimes have to ask a student: "Can you please show us the contract you have where God assigns you the task of judging this person? Where is the piece of paper that proves that you are responsible for this person's salvation?"

This will sometimes make students stop and think. They realize, of course, that they have no such contract. Why have they built the idea that they are responsible for another person's salvation, and they have to act as if they have some kind of ownership over that person?

If you are to pass the initiations at the third level, you must stop seeking to own other people. I am tempted to say that you must shift your focus and seek to gain ownership of yourself, but of course, that is a statement that can easily be misinterpreted. There are indeed many people who have transcended the desire to have ownership of others. They are still seeking ownership of themselves and their own minds, but they are seeking this from the perspective of the ego. They are actually seeking to put their ego in control of their own minds, their thoughts, their feelings, their sense of identity. Rather than seeking ownership of your own mind, I would have you give up any need to own anything on earth.

You cannot confine the Budda Nature to a mental box

What is true wisdom? I have said that the highest wisdom is the awareness that all life is *one* because everything is the Buddha Nature. This was what the Buddha taught so many years ago—twenty-five centuries, a very long time indeed. Look at what people have done to the teachings of the Buddha. They have turned it into an object. You can find various sects that believe they have ownership of the teachings of the Buddha.

My beloved, what is the teaching of the Buddha? Is it a particular outer doctrine expressed in words? If the central realization of Buddhism is that everything is the Buddha Nature, then would it not follow that the teachings of the Buddha are also the Buddha Nature? They have the Buddha Nature within them.

What, then, is the Buddha Nature? People think that the Buddha Nature is some state of perfection, and they think that when something is perfect, it could never change. Ah, here we have the central issue in human existence. The central issue is this: Are you striving towards a state of perfection that you see as non-change, or are you striving for *oneness* with the Buddha Nature?

You see, the Buddha Nature is constant change. The Buddha Nature is constant self-transcendence. The Buddha Nature never stands still. It is constantly transcending itself. What does this mean? It means that you cannot own the Buddha Nature. You cannot control it. You cannot create a mental box and say the Buddha Nature is contained in this box. Before you can even create the mental box, the Buddha Nature has transcended itself a billion times.

God's eye can only see oneness

It is only the human ego who wants to create a state of perfection that does not change because it believes that, when it can create this state of perfection, then it will be acceptable in the eyes of God. As we have said in many teachings, including Jesus' foundational books on the ego, the ego will never be acceptable in the eye of God, for the eye of God sees only oneness, and the eyes of the ego see only separation.

The eye of God sees the reality that all life is the River of Life that is constantly flowing. The eye of oneness will never see the ego, for the ego is apart from oneness, and therefore it is unreal. The eye of oneness can see only that which is real. The eyes of separation can see only that which is unreal and never the twain shall meet. What *can* meet is when the Conscious You steps outside of the perception filter of the ego and experiences oneness, experiences itself as the Buddha Nature, as one with the ever-transcending River of Life. This is wisdom. Wisdom expressed through love is when you realize that you want something more than the illusions of your mental box, of your perception filter. You want the living fount of wisdom, rather than some superior, but static, expression of wisdom.

There are people all over the world who have found a particular spiritual teaching. They have elevated that teaching to the status of superiority, of having some superior authority. They firmly believe that, as long as they keep following that teaching, practicing whatever is prescribed by the teaching or by the outer organization that claims to own the teaching, then they are guaranteed to be saved, enter heaven, become enlightened, enter nirvana or whatever the goal may be.

There are even ascended master students who have taken the teachings of the ascended masters and elevated them to this status of infallibility and superiority, thereby turning them into a closed mental box. They no longer have ears to hear and eyes to see the living teaching that we are. We are one with the Buddha Nature, and we are constantly transcending ourselves, which means that our teachings are constantly transcending themselves.

A mental box is a perversion of love

Only love can help you stay in touch with us as we continue to transcend ourselves, and thereby transcend the teachings that were given in the past, even in the recent past. Take care to note the subtle distinction. A teaching that is given by the ascended masters through a sponsored messenger is a valid teaching. The moment the teaching is given and expressed in the physical realm, we of the ascended masters have already transcended ourselves; and we have transcended the teaching. This does not invalidate the teaching, but it does mean that if you want to stay in touch with us, you cannot turn the teaching into a closed box. You use it as a foundation for transcending both your sense of self and any outer interpretation of the teaching.

What you instead see in ascended master organizations, as you see in all other spiritual and religious organizations, is a certain filtering process. There is often a majority of students who want to take the teaching and turn it into a closed mental box. They do so, and thereby they create an organizational culture that is a closed box. They might even freeze out those who will not accept that organizational culture and its worldview. This minority of the students who are more open, who will not accept the status quo, will move on either to another messenger or to another organization, or they will establish their own inner contact with us so they can receive impulses and teachings directly from us. This is the River of Life. The students who want to stay in a certain box have a perverted form of love. They will claim all day long that they love the ascended masters and they love our teaching. They *do* love us—in a possessive way. They have decided that they have reached a plateau on the spiritual path at which they are very comfortable, and they want us to validate the plateau and them staying at that level. They want us to fit into their mental box, and this is perhaps love but certainly only the human possessive love that has created so many problems on this planet of people seeking to force others, thinking they are doing this with the best of intentions or even with the highest possible authority.

Do you want stagnation or transcendence?

Jesus said: "If you love me, keep my commandments." What was his most important commandment? "He who seeks to save his life shall lose it, but he who is willing to lose his life for my sake shall find it," shall find eternal life in ongoing self-transcendence. The life that Jesus talked about is ongoing self-transcendence. This is the life that the living Christ offers to people in embodiment. If you do not partake of this body and blood of Christ, you have no life in you, for you are seeking to confine your spirit to a mental box defined on earth.

Your spirit cannot fit; therefore it must withdraw and withhold its light and its life from your lower being. If it did not do so, you would create much karma by expressing that light through your perception filter and mental box, using the light from your I AM Presence to force other people and, therefore, make more and more karma for yourself. It is a grace that your I AM Presence withholds the light in order to limit the amount of karma you can make in your attempts to force other people, force the ascended masters, force the entire universe or even force God into your mental box—as the fallen beings have been trying to do for a very long time. There comes a point in your initiations at The Royal Teton Retreat where you must face the absolute necessity of considering what you love. Is there something you love more than your current mental box? Then you must tune in to that something and ask yourself a very serious question: "Do you want greater oneness with that which you love, or do you want to use the perfect arguments, based on your current mental box, to reason against that oneness?" You must come to the point where you see that you face a choice that is like the choice between life and death. Do you want to continue validating your mental box, or do you want greater oneness with that which you love more than the box? You cannot have both.

You cannot have your cake and eat it, too

This is the initiation you face at the third level: You cannot have your cake and eat it, too. Consider the hidden wisdom in this seemingly simple folk saying. You have a piece of cake. You can either sit there and look at it and enjoy the feeling that you have a piece of cake, or you can eat it and then lose the feeling that you own a piece of cake. What is the purpose of cake? Is it that you take the cake and put it on display in a glass cabinet so you can go around showing all your friends and family: "Look at this wonderful cake that I own"? Or is the purpose of the cake that you invite your friends and family, and then you break the cake for them as Christ broke his body for his disciples? You give them each a piece of cake. You have them eat it, and thereby, yes, you do lose the cake. You do lose the sense of owning the cake, but what do you gain instead? You gain oneness with the flow of the River of Life. You gain this oneness because what you have freely received, you are freely giving, and thereby, you are setting yourself free to receive *more*.

    The choice is: You can take your current spiritual teaching and put it into a glass cabinet and walk around and be proud of this wonderful teaching that sits there on display. Or you can break the teaching and eat it, and thereby lose the sense of what you have. Nevertheless, you join the ongoing movement of the ever self-transcending river of teaching that flows from the ascended masters.

You can stand still outside the flow, or you can become one with the flow. You cannot do both. *You cannot do both,* my beloved. Of course, the ego and the false teachers are very anxious to make you believe that you *can* have your cake and eat it too. They want you to believe that, as long as you are studying the teachings from the ascended masters, you are surely moving forward towards your ascension. If you have found a valid messenger that is still bringing forth teachings, then how could you be standing still? You can still be standing still if you are not truly absorbing the teaching and allowing it to take you beyond your mental box.

Even a living teaching that is still flowing can be used to validate your mental box, for your mental box filters out those aspects of the teaching that would challenge the box. If you are not using the teaching to help the Conscious You step outside the mental box, then you will actually use the teaching to solidify the mental box and the belief that this mental box will take you to heaven.

How many times do we need to say that the ascension is not a process whereby you build a mental box that is so perfect that God simply *has* to accept it into the ascended realm? The process of the ascension is a process whereby you shed every aspect of the mental boxes based on separation until you return to your original state of innocence, meaning formlessness. When you transcend all form that says you are this or that, then you can be that which you always were: the formless being that descended. As Jesus said: "No man has ascended back to heaven save he that descended from heaven." Only the pure, formless Conscious You that descended from the spiritual realm can ascend back. This is a mystery to ponder, although it is a bit beyond the third level at the Royal Teton Retreat, but it is a thought that is valid to keep in the back of your mind.

Transcend all ownership if you want to ascend

The Conscious You expands its awareness by being in embodiment, but it does not do so by building a separate sense of self. You are not here to build a separate self so sophisticated that it lives up to some ultimate standard and will be allowed into heaven. You are here to build a separate self, experience life through it for a while, and then transcend that self and continue to do so until you finally have transcended every kind of self that you can think of building in this world. You realize that you are done with experiencing this world. You have transcended all of the selves that you could think of as being valid ways to experience this world of form. Now you are ready to return to formlessness, and it is in this state of formlessness that you ascend.

It is, as they sometimes say about your physical body, that you came into this world naked and you will have to leave it the same way. You cannot take your possessions with you, but you *can* take something with you. What you take with you is not the separate self that you have built. It is the attainment stored in your causal body. This you take with you and this will help you in your ongoing journey as an ascended master.

You do not become an ascended master until you transcend all aspects of the separate self. Everything that you think you own must be transcended. You must give up this life in order to follow Christ, and in order to do that, you must love Christ more than anything in this world. As Jesus said: "He who loves father or mother or brother or sister more than me is not worthy of me." It is indeed true. If you love any aspect of your separate self more than Christ – Christ being ongoing self-transcendence – you are not worthy to be a disciple of Christ because you are not ready to give up everything in order to follow Christ in the ongoing self-transcendence of the River of Life.

The love for expressing your Divine individuality

Love is the greatest motivator, for love is precisely this: self-transcendence. You exist because your Creator desired to be more. You exist in a world that has form because your Creator desired to be more. *You* become more by first identifying yourself with or as a certain form and then transcending that form. It is not the identification that makes you more; it is giving up the identification that makes you more. Giving up is true love, seeking to possess is false love.

We attempt to show our students that they need to give up seeking to own the worldview, the wisdom, the mental box, that they have at their current level. We seek to bring them in touch with what they love more than the security of the mental box. I have talked about loving Christ, for Christ at the personal level is really the expression of your Divine individuality.

I talked about ideal geometric forms. Well, what is your I AM Presence? It is an ideal geometric shape, an intricate geometric shape, and when you begin to glimpse at least a small aspect of that shape, then you will feel the love for wanting to express that shape in this world. You can then see that this cannot be done through your current perception filter and mental box. You have the choice between expressing the individuality in your I AM Presence or clinging to your mental box.

When students come to the point where they see this, and they see how their mental box is limiting them, then you can see how their heart chakra lights up with the intensity of the ruby fire that gives them the determination to literally burn away a particular aspect of their mental box with a laser beam so that they can express more of their divine individuality. This is when they feel divine love flowing through them. When you have as your major goal to express the divine individuality stored in your I AM Presence, what is the need to control other people? What is the need to control yourself and adapt yourself to a particular outer standard on earth?

You need nothing from other people in order to express your Divine individuality. You need nothing from earth in order to express your Divine individuality. You need no particular conditions in the material world in order to express your Divine individuality. You will never be able to express your Divine individuality unless you come to the point where you do it regardless of the outer conditions.

So many students come to us with the attitude that when the outer conditions are just right, then they can express their Christhood. What is the lesson from the embodiment of Jesus? Look at his life! You may think, based on this glorified view created by Christianity, that Jesus had ideal conditions. *But look at his life!* What was the point in the whole story of him being born in a manger because there was no room in the inn? What is the point of him being born out of wedlock, his parents having to flee to Egypt, growing up in humble circumstances? The whole point was to show that even in the most humble and seemingly adverse conditions there can still be an expression of the Christ, of the Buddha Nature, of the divine individuality.

What does it take to express your divine individuality? It does not take that you first seek to create some set of ideal conditions in your life. It takes that you are willing to express your divine individuality *regardless of the outer conditions you face*. This is love. When you look at conditions on earth without looking at them through the judgment of the outer mind and the ego, you do not judge conditions as being less than ideal and say: "I cannot express anything divine in this situation. It is not worthy of this expression."

Passing the initiation through unconditional love

Love is when you take any condition you face, and you find some way to express something more, something that is divine in that situation. That is when you have multiplied the talents, and that is when you will be given more to express. There are those who sit around having a spiritual teaching, having some understanding of the spiritual path, but they are sitting around waiting for some ideal condition to occur when they will suddenly, automatically, express the Christ or something spiritual. There are those who go into whatever situation they face, and they find ways to express a higher reality in that situation.

Those are the ones who multiply their talents instead of burying them in the ground. Those are the ones who pass the initiation at the third level of The Royal Teton Retreat, that of being willing to express love in any condition even if it seems to be unworthy of love, even if it seems that it is impossible to express love in this condition. You are even expressing love towards those people who do not seem to deserve love, who do not seem to want love, who do not seem willing to receive it. You express love even if people put you down or put your love down, even if they trample it under foot and ridicule it in the most vile manner. You still give expression to what is coming from within. You are being the sun, the open door for the sun of your I AM Presence to shine through to the material world. *That* is your role; *that* is why you are here.

When your love is great enough that you can express the Divine regardless of what other people do with it, then you have developed the motivation that is based on love. Then you have passed that initiation at the third level, and you can move on to the fourth. Then you have developed the non-judgmentalness that allows you to accelerate your motives to a higher level of purity where you have pure intentions.

This will, of course, be the topic of my next discourse. For now, I leave you to ponder the question: "Do you want to *have* your cake, or do you want to eat it and join the River of Life?" Lanto, I AM!

9 | I INVOKE LOVE-BASED MOTIVATION

In the name I AM THAT I AM, Jesus Christ, I call to my I AM Presence to flow through the I Will Be Presence that I AM and give this invocation with full power. I call to beloved Elohim Apollo and Lumina and Heros and Amora, Archangel Jophiel and Christine and Chamuel and Charity, Master Lanto and Paul the Venetian to help me purify my motivation from all possessive love and develop a motivation based on the love for expressing my Divine individuality. Help me see and surrender all patterns that block my oneness with Master Lanto and my oneness with my I AM Presence, including …

[Make personal calls]

1. I love wisdom more than my ego

1. Master Lanto, help me go deep within and reconnect to the love that is beyond my current mental box, the love that brought the Conscious You to take embodiment in the material universe.

Beloved Apollo, with your second ray,
you open my eyes to see a new day,
I see through duality's lies and deceit,
transcending the mindset producing defeat.

**Beloved Apollo, thou Elohim Gold,
your radiant light my eyes now behold,
as pages of wisdom you gently unfold,
I feel I am free from all that is old.**

2. Master Lanto, help me reconnect to the love for seeing God's creation unfold, the love for my I AM Presence, the love for my particular individualized God qualities, the love for expressing those God qualities, seeing that light radiating in the darkness of the material realm.

Beloved Apollo, in your flame I know,
that your living wisdom is always a flow,
in your light I see my own highest will,
immersed in the stream that never stands still.

**Beloved Apollo, your light makes it clear,
why we have taken embodiment here,
working to raise our own cosmic sphere,
together we form the tip of the spear.**

3. Master Lanto, help me reconnect to the love that brought me to this planet and help me see how I can express love with greater wisdom, with greater discernment.

Beloved Apollo, exposing all lies,
I hereby surrender all ego-based ties,
I know my perception is truly the key,
to transcending the serpentine duality.

> **Beloved Apollo, we heed now your call,**
> **drawing us into Wisdom's Great Hall,**
> **exposing all lies causing the fall,**
> **you help us reclaim the oneness of all.**

4. Master Lanto, help me see that what people do with wisdom on earth is not driven by Divine Love; it is driven by human love.

> Beloved Apollo, your wisdom so clear,
> in oneness with you, no serpent I fear,
> the beam in my eye I'm willing to see,
> I'm free from the serpent's own duality.

> **Beloved Apollo, my eyes now I raise,**
> **I see that the Earth is in a new phase,**
> **I willingly stand in your piercing gaze,**
> **empowered, I exit duality's maze.**

5. I surrender all tendency to use wisdom as the basis for judgment, including value judgment. True Divine Wisdom gives me discernment, but discernment has nothing to do with human judgment.

> O Heros-Amora, in your love so pink,
> I care not what others about me may think,
> in oneness with you, I claim a new day,
> an innocent child, I frolic and play.

> **O Heros-Amora, a new life begun,**
> **I laugh at the devil, the serious one,**
> **I bathe in your glorious Ruby-Pink Sun,**
> **knowing my God allows life to be fun.**

6. Master Lanto, help me see the difference between Christ discernment and the judgment that springs from the mind of anti-Christ.

> O Heros-Amora, life is such a joy,
> I see that the world is like a great toy,
> whatever my mind into it projects,
> the mirror of life exactly reflects.

> **O Heros-Amora, I reap what I sow,**
> **yet this is Plan B for helping me grow,**
> **for truly, Plan A is that I join the flow,**
> **immersed in the Infinite Love you bestow.**

7. Master Lanto, help me see if I have used an ascended master teaching to build a mental box that is as closed as the mental box of many fundamentalist Christian groups.

> O Heros-Amora, conditions you burn,
> I know I AM free to take a new turn,
> Immersed in the stream of infinite Love,
> I know that my Spirit came from Above.

> **O Heros-Amora, awakened I see,**
> **in true love is no conditionality,**
> **the devil is stuck in his duality,**
> **but I AM set free by Love's reality.**

8. Master Lanto, help me experience the difference in vibration between Christ discernment and human judgment. I am passing the initiations at the third level, the initiations of wisdom expressed through love.

9 | I Invoke Love-based Motivation

O Heros-Amora, I feel that at last,
I've risen above the trap of my past,
in true love I claim my freedom to grow,
forever I'm one with Love's Infinite Flow.

**O Heros-Amora, conditions are ties,
forming a net of serpentine lies,
your love has no bounds, forever it flies,
raising all life into Ruby-Pink skies.**

9. Love does not judge. Divine Love does not judge, but human love is entirely based on a judgment.

Accelerate my Awakeness, I AM real,
Accelerate my Awakeness, all life heal,
Accelerate my Awakeness, I AM MORE,
Accelerate my Awakeness, all will soar.

Accelerate my Awakeness! (3X)
Beloved Apollo and Lumina.
Accelerate my Awakeness! (3X)
Beloved Jophiel and Christine.
Accelerate my Awakeness! (3X)
Beloved Master Lanto.
Accelerate my Awakeness! (3X)
Beloved I AM.

2. I am ready to transcend ownership

1. Master Lanto, help me see and surrender all tendency to use human, possessive love to seek to own or control another person.

Jophiel Archangel, in wisdom's great light,
all serpentine lies exposed to my sight.
So subtle the lies that creep through the mind,
yet you are the greatest teacher I find.

**Jophiel Archangel, exposing all lies,
Jophiel Archangel, cutting all ties.
Jophiel Archangel, clearing the skies,
Jophiel Archangel, my mind truly flies.**

2. Master Lanto, help me see and surrender the illusion that it could ever be for another person's good that I seek to force the free will of that person. God never appointed me as the judge of how other people should exercise their free will.

Jophiel Archangel, your wisdom I hail,
your sword cutting through duality's veil.
As you show the way, I know what is real,
from serpentine doubt, I instantly heal.

**Jophiel Archangel, exposing all lies,
Jophiel Archangel, cutting all ties.
Jophiel Archangel, clearing the skies,
Jophiel Archangel, my mind truly flies.**

3. Master Lanto, show me how I am exercising conditional love, possessive love, in my relationships with other people.

Jophiel Archangel, your reality,
the best antidote to duality.
No lie can remain in your Presence so clear,
with you on my side, no serpent I fear.

**Jophiel Archangel, exposing all lies,
Jophiel Archangel, cutting all ties.
Jophiel Archangel, clearing the skies,
Jophiel Archangel, my mind truly flies.**

4. I acknowledge that I have no contract where God assigns me the task of judging another person. I have no piece of paper that proves that I am responsible for another person's salvation.

Jophiel Archangel, God's mind is in me,
and through your clear light, its wisdom I see.
Divisions all vanish, as I see the One,
and truly, the wholeness of mind I have won.

**Jophiel Archangel, exposing all lies,
Jophiel Archangel, cutting all ties.
Jophiel Archangel, clearing the skies,
Jophiel Archangel, my mind truly flies.**

5. I surrender the illusion that I am responsible for another person's salvation. I surrender the ego's tendency to seek ownership over other people.

Chamuel Archangel, in ruby ray power,
I know I am taking a life-giving shower.
Love burning away all perversions of will,
I suddenly feel my desires falling still.

**Chamuel Archangel, descend from Above,
Chamuel Archangel, with ruby-pink love,
Chamuel Archangel, so often thought-of,
Chamuel Archangel, o come Holy Dove.**

6. Master Lanto, help me see if I am seeking ownership of myself and my own mind from the perspective of the ego, seeking to put my ego in control of my thoughts, feelings and sense of identity.

> Chamuel Archangel, a spiral of light,
> as ruby ray fire now pierces the night.
> All forces of darkness consumed by your fire,
> consuming all those who will not rise higher.

> **Chamuel Archangel, descend from Above,**
> **Chamuel Archangel, with ruby-pink love,**
> **Chamuel Archangel, so often thought-of,**
> **Chamuel Archangel, o come Holy Dove.**

7. Master Lanto, I am willing to give up any need to own anything on earth. Show me the way to the state where I own no thing and no thing owns me.

> Chamuel Archangel, your love so immense,
> with clarified vision, my life now makes sense.
> The purpose of life you so clearly reveal,
> immersed in your love, God's oneness I feel.

> **Chamuel Archangel, descend from Above,**
> **Chamuel Archangel, with ruby-pink love,**
> **Chamuel Archangel, so often thought-of,**
> **Chamuel Archangel, o come Holy Dove.**

8. Master Lanto, help me attain the awareness that all life is *one* because everything is the Buddha Nature.

Chamuel Archangel, what calmness you bring,
I see now that even death has no sting.
For truly, in love there can be no decay,
as love is transcendence into a new day.

**Chamuel Archangel, descend from Above,
Chamuel Archangel, with ruby-pink love,
Chamuel Archangel, so often thought-of,
Chamuel Archangel, o come Holy Dove.**

9. Master Lanto, help me overcome the tendency to think that the Buddha Nature is a state of perfection that does not change. Help me transcend the ego's drive for a state of perfection that is non-change. I am striving for *oneness* with the Buddha Nature.

With angels I soar,
as I reach for MORE.
The angels so real,
their love all will heal.
The angels bring peace,
all conflicts will cease.
With angels of light,
we soar to new height.

**The rustling sound of angel wings,
what joy as even matter sings,
what joy as every atom rings,
in harmony with angel wings.**

3. I am expressing wisdom through love

1. The Buddha Nature is constant change. The Buddha Nature is constant self-transcendence. The Buddha Nature never stands still. It is constantly transcending itself.

> Master Lanto, golden wise,
> expose in me the ego's lies.
> Master Lanto, will to be,
> I will to win my mastery.

**O Holy Spirit, flow through me,
I am the open door for thee.
O mighty rushing stream of Light,
transcendence is my sacred right.**

2. I cannot own the Buddha Nature. I cannot control it. I cannot create a mental box and say the Buddha Nature is contained in this box. Before I can even create the mental box, the Buddha Nature has transcended itself a billion times.

> Master Lanto, balance all,
> for wisdom's balance I do call.
> Master Lanto, help me see,
> that balance is the Golden key.

**O Holy Spirit, flow through me,
I am the open door for thee.
O mighty rushing stream of Light,
transcendence is my sacred right.**

3. It is only the human ego who wants to create a state of perfection that does not change because it believes this will make it acceptable in the eyes of God.

Master Lanto, from Above,
I call forth discerning love.
Master Lanto, love's not blind,
through love, God vision I will find.

**O Holy Spirit, flow through me,
I am the open door for thee.
O mighty rushing stream of Light,
transcendence is my sacred right.**

4. Master Lanto, help me, as the Conscious You, step outside the perception filter of the ego and experience oneness, experience myself as the Buddha Nature, as one with the ever-transcending River of Life.

Master Lanto, pure I am,
intentions pure as Christic lamb.
Master Lanto, I will transcend,
acceleration now my truest friend.

**O Holy Spirit, flow through me,
I am the open door for thee.
O mighty rushing stream of Light,
transcendence is my sacred right.**

5. Wisdom expressed through love is when I realize that I want something more than the illusions of my mental box, my perception filter. I want the living fount of wisdom, rather than a static expression of wisdom.

Master Lanto, I am whole,
no more division in my soul.
Master Lanto, healing flame,
all balance in your sacred name.

> O Holy Spirit, flow through me,
> I am the open door for thee.
> O mighty rushing stream of Light,
> transcendence is my sacred right.

6. Master Lanto, I realize the ascended masters are constantly transcending themselves. I want to stay in touch with you, and I am using the outer teachings as the foundation for transcending both my sense of self and any interpretation of the teaching.

> Master Lanto, serve all life,
> as I transcend all inner strife.
> Master Lanto, peace you give,
> to all who want to truly live.

> O Holy Spirit, flow through me,
> I am the open door for thee.
> O mighty rushing stream of Light,
> transcendence is my sacred right.

7. The life that Jesus talked about is ongoing self-transcendence. This is the life that the living Christ offers to people in embodiment. I am partaking of this body and blood of Christ, and I surrender all desire to confine my spirit to a mental box defined on earth.

> Master Lanto, free to be,
> in balanced creativity.
> Master Lanto, we employ,
> your balance as the key to joy.

> O Holy Spirit, flow through me,
> I am the open door for thee.
> O mighty rushing stream of Light,
> transcendence is my sacred right.

8. Master Lanto, help me see how I am expressing spiritual light through my perception filter and mental box. I surrender the tendency to use the light from my I AM Presence to force other people and make karma for myself.

> Master Lanto, balance all,
> the seven rays upon my call.
> Master Lanto, I take flight,
> my threefold flame a blazing light.

> O Holy Spirit, flow through me,
> I am the open door for thee.
> O mighty rushing stream of Light,
> transcendence is my sacred right.

9. I love Master Lanto more than my current mental box. I want greater oneness with Lanto and my I AM Presence. I surrender all desire to use the arguments based on my current mental box to reason against that oneness. I choose life!

> Lanto dear, your Presence here,
> filling up my inner sphere.
> Life is now a sacred flow,
> God Wisdom I on all bestow.

> O Holy Spirit, flow through me,
> I am the open door for thee.
> O mighty rushing stream of Light,
> transcendence is my sacred right.

4. My motivation is love-based

1. I am willing to transcend everything that I think I own. I become more by identifying myself with form and then transcending form. It is not the identification that makes me more; it is giving up the identification that makes me more.

> Master Paul, venetian dream,
> your love for beauty's flowing stream.
> Master Paul, in love's own womb,
> your power shatters ego's tomb.
>
> **O Holy Spirit, flow through me,**
> **I am the open door for thee.**
> **O mighty rushing stream of Light,**
> **transcendence is my sacred right.**

2. Giving up is true love, seeking to possess is false love. What I love more than anything in this world is the expression of my Divine individuality. I love the ideal geometric forms of my I AM Presence.

> Master Paul, your counsel wise,
> my mind is raised to lofty skies.
> Master Paul, in wisdom's love,
> such beauty flowing from Above.
>
> **O Holy Spirit, flow through me,**
> **I am the open door for thee.**
> **O mighty rushing stream of Light,**
> **transcendence is my sacred right.**

3. With the intensity and determination of the ruby fire, I am burning away a particular aspect of my mental box with a laser beam. I am expressing more of my divine individuality, I am feeling divine love flowing through me.

> Master Paul, love is an art,
> it opens up the secret heart.
> Master Paul, love's rushing flow,
> my heart awash in sacred glow.

**O Holy Spirit, flow through me,
I am the open door for thee.
O mighty rushing stream of Light,
transcendence is my sacred right.**

4. My major goal is to express the divine individuality stored in my I AM Presence. I surrender all need to control other people. I surrender the need to control myself and adapt myself to a particular outer standard on earth.

> Master Paul, accelerate,
> upon pure love I meditate.
> Master Paul, intentions pure,
> my self-transcendence will ensure.

**O Holy Spirit, flow through me,
I am the open door for thee.
O mighty rushing stream of Light,
transcendence is my sacred right.**

5. I need nothing from other people in order to express my Divine individuality. I need nothing from earth in order to express my Divine individuality. I need no particular conditions in the material world in order to express my Divine individuality.

Master Paul, your love will heal,
my inner light you do reveal.
Master Paul, all life console,
with you I'm being truly whole.

**O Holy Spirit, flow through me,
I am the open door for thee.
O mighty rushing stream of Light,
transcendence is my sacred right.**

6. I am willing to express my divine individuality regardless of the outer conditions I face. I take any condition I face, and I find some way to express something more, something that is divine, in that situation.

Master Paul, you serve the All,
by helping us transcend the fall.
Master Paul, in peace we rise,
as ego meets its sure demise.

**O Holy Spirit, flow through me,
I am the open door for thee.
O mighty rushing stream of Light,
transcendence is my sacred right.**

7. I am expressing love in any condition even if it seems to be unworthy of love, even if it seems that it is impossible to express love in this condition. I am expressing love towards people who do not seem to deserve love, who do not want love.

Master Paul, love all life free,
your love is for eternity.
Master Paul, you are the One,
to help us make the journey fun.

> O Holy Spirit, flow through me,
> I am the open door for thee.
> O mighty rushing stream of Light,
> transcendence is my sacred right.

8. I give expression to what is coming from within. I AM being the sun, the open door for the sun of my I AM Presence to shine through to the material world. *That* is my role; *that* is why I am here.

> Master Paul, you balance all,
> the seven rays upon my call.
> Master Paul, you paint the sky,
> with colors that delight the I.

> O Holy Spirit, flow through me,
> I am the open door for thee.
> O mighty rushing stream of Light,
> transcendence is my sacred right.

9. My love is great enough that I can express the Divine regardless of what other people do with it. I have developed a motivation that is based on love.

> Master Paul, your Presence here,
> filling up my inner sphere.
> Life is now a sacred flow,
> God Love I do on all bestow.

> O Holy Spirit, flow through me,
> I am the open door for thee.
> O mighty rushing stream of Light,
> transcendence is my sacred right.

Sealing:

In the name of the Divine Mother, I fully accept that the power of these calls is used to set free the Ma-ter light, so it can outpicture the perfect vision of Christ for my own life, for all people and for the planet. In the name I AM THAT I AM, it is done! Amen.

10 | WISDOM AND PURITY

I AM the Ascended Master Lanto. I come to give you some thoughts on the initiations that students go through at the fourth level of the Royal Teton Retreat. These are the initiations of the Fourth Ray, meaning wisdom expressed through purity or acceleration. "Purity" means purity of intention, and what we seek to help students attain at this level is clarity about their intentions for using wisdom.

When students come to my retreat, they have the typical desire that is so prevalent on earth. This is the desire that is fueled by the ego's quest for security in this world. People blinded by this desire are seeking to find a kind of wisdom that they can elevate to some status of infallibility. If your wisdom is infallible, then your security must be at its maximum, or so the ego reasons. This means that students tend to use wisdom in order to validate what makes their ego's feel secure. The difficult task I face at this level is to get students to see the hollowness of this approach.

I seek to help students see how illogical this is, how hypocritical it is. People who are trapped in this desire to validate the ego will claim that they have the highest possible motives for their use of wisdom. They believe they have an absolute and infallible expression of wisdom, and it is in the interest of other people and in the interest of some higher cause, possibly even the cause of God himself, that they seek to force their wisdom upon others.

They claim they have an absolute form of wisdom. In reality, their wisdom is entirely relative. It is completely relative to what their egos have accepted and to a sense of security that the ego has built. As we have said many times before, the ego can never find absolute security. It seeks to build security in this world, but it will always be a house built on sand because nothing in this world can be unchangeable. Of course, nothing in the spiritual world is unchangeable either, and therefore the dream of some static state of perfection or security is nothing but an empty dream. This, of course, the ego can never see.

Absolute security in the River of Life

The Conscious You, however, *can* experience this by experiencing pure awareness. Hereby, it realizes that its own nature is an absolute state of security—not in the sense that it is unchanging, but in the sense that it is ever-transcending. Or rather, we could say that at the core of your being is that which is unchanging, namely awareness, and once you connect to that unchanging awareness, you then find security in constantly transcending the outer expressions of awareness, what your awareness is focused upon. You, therefore, do not need to stop the flow of the River of Life in order to feel secure; you feel secure in flowing with it. This is absolute or ultimate security, but it is security through self-transcendence. It is the security that is ever-flowing.

What have I said about the River of Life? It is constantly transcending itself. What have I said about Divine Wisdom? It is constantly transcending itself. Nothing, therefore, stands still—certainly, not the fount of living wisdom. This, again, means that the ego is on an impossible quest of seeking to create a static expression of wisdom that can never be changed, that can never be threatened, that can never be overturned. As we have explained with the second law of thermodynamics, anything that becomes a closed system *will* break down because its own internal contradictions will increase the chaos that breaks it down.

The fourth initiation of the Second Ray

The reality is that the harder a student is trying to maintain the outer security of its ego, the more the student will generate energy impulses that are sent into the cosmic mirror. These energy impulses will be returned as conditions that seek to threaten the student's sense of security. The student must, therefore, send more powerful impulses to counteract this return, and this, of course, generates an even stronger return. This "arms race" can go on until the student breaks under the strain and can no longer do this.

We, of course, seek to help people see the fallacy of this before they break under the strain, but there are some students who come to our retreat and have to go through that process of breaking. They realize that they do not have the force, the power, to counteract the threats to their sense of security. What must you then do? You must give up; you must surrender. There is no other step.

The acceleration of the Fourth Ray is not the same as accumulation. You might think that if you need to generate an energy impulse to counteract something that is coming at you, then you need to accumulate more and more power, more and more material, physical power. As I have said, accumulating more power only means that you generate a more powerful impulse coming at you in the future.

Acceleration means that you go beyond accumulating power at a certain level because you accelerate your vibration to a higher level where you are no longer feeling the lower energies, that you generated in the past, when they are returned to you by the cosmic mirror. They pass right through you. They are insignificant to you. They are irrelevant to your life experience. This is true acceleration, and in this there is security in the sense that you go beyond the past.

Even ascended master teachings are relative

In order to help students pass this level of initiation, we seek to help them see that the wisdom, the thought systems, created by the ego – and created by human beings and created by the false teachers – are truly relative, even though they claim to be absolute. They are relative because they are relative to the duality consciousness, and therefore they are relative to an opposite. For every expression of wisdom that springs from the duality consciousness, there is an opposite. This is not easy to understand for most students, even though we have taken them through the steps, as I have explained before, of teaching them how words can be interpreted and misinterpreted. It is still difficult for people to grasp, and the difficulty is understandable.

When I say that any expression of "wisdom" that comes from the duality consciousness has an opposite, this is true; yet, it is equally true that any expression of wisdom that comes from the ascended masters also has an opposite. The difference is that when wisdom is expressed through the duality consciousness, the opposition is built in because there is a contradiction in the way the dualistic consciousness looks at the world.

What we give at the ascended level has no internal contradiction, but of course, as soon as we give a teaching, the false teachers and their students will come up with an opposition to that teaching; and thus any expression given in words has an opposite. Any expression given in words can be counteracted, or neutralized, or invalidated, or at least contradicted by another statement made with words. This is an inevitable consequence of the fact that the collective consciousness on earth is still so low that most people are blinded by the duality consciousness. When you are looking at an ascended master teaching through the perception filter of the outer self, the separate self, you can easily see an opposite to the ascended master teaching.

You may still accept that teaching, but what you are actually doing is that you are seeking to use it to validate your ego's need for security by elevating it, and the expression of the teaching, to some status of infallibility. What have I said? I have said that you should never focus on the words so that you forget the spirit behind the words. It is essential for you to connect to my Presence, to the flow of wisdom, the living Spirit of Wisdom. You cannot do that if you take a certain worded expression of wisdom and elevate it to the status of infallibility, meaning you never want to change it or you never want to go beyond it. This is not acceleration; this is an attempt to build an accumulation that has the appearance of authority. We aim to show students that any expression of wisdom that springs from the duality consciousness, or that has been interpreted through the duality consciousness, is relative.

Even ascended master students have used our teachings to build a relative worldview. The importance of this is that something that is relative is not absolute wisdom. This is often difficult for students to understand because they are still so attached to the ego's desire to build ultimate security. It takes a major adjustment for students to overcome this. In fact, it takes that they begin to experience pure awareness until they experience that they can find this inner security instead of the outer security of an absolute or infallible belief system.

Even many ascended master students cling to the belief that if they are a member of a certain organization or follow a certain teaching given by this highest possible messenger, then they are guaranteed to make their ascension. They are very reluctant to let go of this belief, which is why some of them are stuck in organizations that no longer have a functioning messenger and do not have the flow of the living word. They cling to the teachings given in the past, and although those teachings are timeless and valid, they are not an expression of where the ascended masters are at in consciousness today. We have transcended ourselves many times since the teachings were given, but of course, the worded expression cannot transcend itself, especially not when it has been elevated to the status of being perfect or infallible. For those students who are willing to give up this need for outer security, we can help them take a major step forward by seeing that any worded expression will be relative.

A description with words is not a direct experience

Words have different meanings to different people so words are interpreted. We have used this example before, but I will use it again. Imagine that you are standing on the beach with a person who has been blind from birth. You are looking at the sunset, and now your task is to describe the sunset to the blind person. Normally, you would try to refer to something that the person has experienced, but the person has never seen with physical eyes. How would you describe the sunset to a blind person? You can do it through words, but what will the blind person get out of that? The person will get a *description* of a sunset.

It may be a very good description, a very accurate description, but for the blind person, it is only a description, not a direct experience. When we give you wisdom from the ascended realm, we are experiencing the Spirit of Wisdom. When we translate that experience into words, it becomes a description of the spirit, not the spirit. This is not a matter of how good the messenger is; it is simply an inevitable consequence of translating an experience into words. Words can only convey a description. What is the difference? It is that a description is needed only when you do not have the direct experience. A description is needed only when there is distance, when there is separation, between you and the experience. You, in embodiment, are like the blind person who has never experienced the Spirit of Wisdom. We are giving you a description of that spirit with words, but in your mind, it can only be a description. Which means what? It means that the very fact that you are separated from the spirit means that you can only grasp a description of the spirit. The more you focus your attention on the description, the more it will actually close your mind to a direct experience.

The purpose of giving spiritual teachings

Our goal for giving teachings is not to get our students to have this wonderful description of the spirit. Our goal is to give our students a direct experience of the spirit. I am the Chohan of the Second Ray. I am not interested in having students on earth who have the most elaborate description of the Second Ray. I am interested in having students on earth who are able to open their minds so that the Spirit of the Second Ray is streaming through their minds, and they are experiencing that spirit as the spirit is being expressed through them. *That* is what I want.

I do not want students who take a worded description and use it to close their minds to the experience. I want you to take the description and use it as a stepping stone for opening your mind to the direct experience. This is my goal. How will you attain this? By overcoming your attachment to a particular worded expression of wisdom and realizing that an expression of wisdom is only a description, and it has value only if you use it to open your mind to a direct experience of the spirit behind the words. When you come to this point, when you come to this realization, you can begin to take the next step. What will it take for you to be an open door for the Spirit of Wisdom to flow through you?

What is a spirit? Again, you have the false images of God created by the major religions of the world that portray God as a static, perfect being sitting up in heaven. God is not static. God is the ever-flowing, ever-transcending spirit—this is the Creator. How do you get to know the spirit? Not through a description whereby you look at it from a distance. You will know the spirit when you overcome distance between yourself and the spirit, when you come into gnosis with the spirit, when you become an open door so that the spirit flows through you.

How can you allow the spirit to flow through you? You cannot do so if you cling to a static expression in words and demand that the spirit conform to or validate that expression. If you are imposing a restriction on the spirit, how will you experience the flow of the spirit? If you are saying that the spirit should not flow but should validate a static expression, then you have lost the spirit.

Accelerate yourself beyond any worded expression

I have said that any expression of wisdom coming from the duality consciousness is relative. An expression of wisdom that comes from the duality consciousness is relative to another expression of wisdom coming from the duality consciousness. Even though human beings may project that one of those expressions is false and one is true, one is right one is wrong, this has no reality to it. Neither of these expressions will help you accelerate yourself beyond the level of the duality consciousness.

Here comes the subtlety where you need to be more sophisticated than most people, even than most ascended master students. An expression of wisdom that comes from the ascended realm is also relative. Even a dictation given by us through a sponsored messenger is not an absolute expression of truth. It is a relative expression, but an expression coming from our level is not relative to an opposite in the material realm. It is relative to the spirit, and therefore, if you follow our expression beyond the words, you end up with the spirit. If you take a dualistic expression and follow it beyond the words, you also end up with a spirit. It is a spirit in the material frequency spectrum, and it cannot help you transcend to the ascended level.

When you follow the words coming from an ascended master to their source, you end up at that master and the spirit of that master, and this can help you accelerate yourself beyond the level of duality. This is the difference. This is the Alpha aspect of saying that even a dictation from ascended masters is relative, but there is an Omega aspect of this as well. Any expression given from us is relative to a particular level of consciousness in which people are trapped. It is adapted to that level because our goal is not to give forth an ultimate or infallible expression of wisdom. We know this cannot be done with words.

Our goal is to give an expression of wisdom that is adapted to people at a certain level of consciousness in a certain mental box, and it gives them what they need to accelerate themselves beyond that particular mental box. We are not seeking to give people something that will take them to the ultimate stage. We are seeking to take them one step beyond. This is the very essence of the path of initiation. At the fourth level of my retreat, the ultimate initiation you need to pass is that you realize what the path of initiation is all about.

The essence of the path of initiation

When you are at a certain level, be it the 48th or the 2nd or the 142nd, your concern is not to pass some ultimate test or acquire some ultimate wisdom. Your task is to take the very next step up the spiral staircase. Your task is to pass the very next initiation that takes you to the level above where you are at right now. In order to do that, you need to acquire the wisdom that challenges your current mental box so that you can accelerate yourself beyond it.

This is the highest wisdom. The highest wisdom is always the wisdom that you can grasp with you present level of consciousness but that can still accelerate you to the next level up. *That,* my beloved, is ultimate wisdom, but that wisdom is naturally relative to both the level of consciousness where you are at and the level of consciousness that is immediately above where you are at.

If you will, you can say that there *is* an ultimate level of wisdom. That is the level you can receive at the 144th level of consciousness, which then accelerates you to the ascended state. What would be the point in giving you that wisdom when you are at the 58th level where you cannot possibly grasp that wisdom? You have no way to make use of it because you cannot relate it to your present level of consciousness. You need to have a form of wisdom that is relative to your present level of consciousness so you can relate it to your present situation but that is also relative to the level above so you can accelerate yourself to that level.

Let go of the desire for an ultimate teaching

If you are to pass the Fourth Ray initiations at the Royal Teton Retreat, you need to give up this ego-based desire for acquiring some ultimate form of wisdom and then going out and impressing other people with your superior wisdom. It is a completely futile desire; it is a futile quest. Can you see this? Can you grasp this? Can you feel the opposition from your ego and possibly from the false teachers who howl at you that what I am giving you *must* be a false teaching, that you should not accept it because it will take you to hell? This must come from a false hierarchy impostor and not a real ascended master.

This is what they will project at you, and there are many students who have allowed their conscious minds to go into a fear mode. They reject the very ideas that could take them to the next level of consciousness. There are many ascended master students who cling to the belief that some expression, some messenger, some organization, has given forth an ultimate teaching. This is, of course, as it should be because these students must have that experience for a while longer. They need to take it to some ultimate extreme before they have finally had enough of it and can let it go. I am not giving a teaching that I expect everyone to grasp. I am giving a teaching for those who are ready for it, for they are ready to pass that initiation at the fourth level and grasp and accept that initiation with their conscious minds.

It is such a relief for you when you let go of this desire to find the ultimate teaching, for then you also transcend the fear of having a false teaching. So many students, whether they are in an ascended master teaching or another spiritual or religious teaching, are so afraid of accepting false ideas that they dare not consider true ideas. Their minds are not open. They are closed to anything that goes beyond the belief system that they have elevated to the status of superiority and infallibility.

My beloved, can you see the irony? If you are aware of the existence of ascended masters and accept that we exist, can you not realize that we are ascended? We exist in the *ascended* realm. How do you ascend? By transcending *everything* on earth. What sense does it then make to say that we as ascended masters should conform to a belief system on earth? What sense does it make to say that we who are the ascended masters should conform to a belief system that we have given to human beings in the past?

How can you take our past dictations, given through one valid messenger, and use them as a weapon against all future messengers? You are using them as a weapon against *us* to prevent us from reaching you with a higher expression of wisdom adapted to the current age or a higher level of consciousness. Does this really make sense? Does it really make sense to be so afraid of false ideas, so afraid of the false hierarchy and the false teachers, that you close your mind to all teachers, even the true teachers of the ascended masters?

The difference between true and false students

Again, this is a matter of motivation, of accelerating your intention. What is your intention for acquiring wisdom? Is it to validate the ego and its need for security or is it to transcend your present level of consciousness? If you want to transcend your present level of consciousness, you can do it in only one way: by making direct contact with spiritual teachers who are beyond your present level.

This is another aspect of the path of initiation that you need to understand. There are, unfortunately, many spiritual people, even many ascended master students, who believe that if only they acquire some superior expression of wisdom expressed in words, then that formula, that worded expression, that scripture, that sacred text, will automatically propel them to a higher state of consciousness.

This has never been the case. This is what is sought by the false hierarchy impostors and by the students of those impostors who seek, through magic, to get some automatic mastery, the false mastery of those who seek to take heaven by force because they are not willing to let their separate selves, their ego-based selves die. They are not willing to look at the beam in their own eye, and they think they can acquire special powers without having to give up the ego so that they can gain power over others or impress others.

These are not the true students, for the true students want to raise up themselves first of all, but they also want to raise up all life. These are the true students of Christ, and when you raise your intention, you are not acquiring wisdom in order to validate your ego's need for security. You are not acquiring wisdom to impress others. You are not acquiring it to get some special powers that can impress others or get you what you want here in the material realm. You are seeking wisdom that can help you accelerate yourself to the next level of consciousness but that can also help you inspire others to go through that acceleration. You are seeking to raise up yourself and to raise up others, thereby, raising all life. This is the true motivation for acquiring wisdom.

You are not seeking to acquire some ultimate or absolute wisdom. You are seeking to acquire a wisdom that is useful for yourself to transcend your level but also useful for inspiring others to transcend their level, whatever it may be that you have encountered in your embodiment on earth. This means that you do not go out and hammer people with some superior wisdom, demanding that they accept this.

You look at people openly and honestly and consider where they are in consciousness. Then, you seek to give them something that will take them one step higher—not two-hundred steps higher in one giant leap, but one step higher. When they have taken that step, you might give them more, but you do not give them all of it at once. This is not wisdom. This is what people do when they are blinded by their egos where it becomes an all or nothing. "You must either accept the fullness of our superior belief system or go to hell," as the Christians have now been hammering at people for so many centuries that more and more people are getting so fed up with the message that they completely reject the spirit behind Christianity, namely Jesus himself.

How will you ever receive the wisdom of an ascended master unless you go beyond the words and experience the spirit of that master—the living, the ever-flowing, ever-transcending spirit of the master? How will you experience that living spirit if you demand that the spirit conforms to some past expression in words that are now frozen in matter? Once a word is expressed, it is frozen, but the spirit is never frozen. What do you want: a frozen expression of words or the living fount of the spirit?

There is no failed experiment on the spiritual path

That is your choice at the fourth level. Sometimes, it takes students a very, very long time to make the choice that they want the spirit more than anything else. When they finally do make the choice, they realize that, by accelerating their intention and by being willing to continually accelerate their intention, they actually accelerate themselves away from the false teachers, the false hierarchy impostors, and their false teaching.

What does it matter if you have accepted a false teaching if you are continually seeking to accelerate yourself? You will then come to see that it was false, and in seeing that it was false, you have accelerated yourself and acquired discernment. Now you know what does not work. You have, of course, heard the story of Thomas Edison seeking the right material for the light bulb. He discovered a thousand ways *not* to make a light bulb. Each of those experiments was not a failed experiment; it was a successful experiment. It showed him: "Ah! This does not work."

What is the process of the ascension? It is that you discover one thousand ways *not* to make an ascended master. For each way you discover *not* to make an ascended master, you take one step up. Finally, you are at the step where you can discover the *one* way to *make* an ascended master—and then you *are* an ascended master.

There is no such thing as a failed experiment on the path of the ascension. Whether it works or it doesn't work, you can learn from it and accelerate yourself to a higher level of consciousness. *That* is the mark of a true student; *not* that you demand some guarantee that if you follow this outer teaching or this outer guru, then you will make your ascension. No, you are willing to experiment for you are beginning to realize that the key to making the ascension is to make contact with the spirit, to become the open door for the spirit, to become one with the spirit.

What is an ascended master? I am the Chohan of the Second Ray, not because I have *studied* the Second Ray and have knowledge from a distance of the Second Ray. I am the Chohan of the Second Ray because *I am one* with the spirit of the Second Ray. Therefore, *I am* the Second Ray. I have risen to a level where I no longer see myself as being one with the Second Ray, for *I am* the Second Ray!

I *am* the representative of the Second Ray for earth. There is none other. There is no spirit that is flowing through me. *I am* the spirit that is flowing, and my spirit is willing to flow through you, if you will open yourself up to the flow that will help you transcend your current level, whatever level that might be, by challenging your current mental box.

If you are willing to be challenged, I am willing to challenge. We can both flow to a higher level, we can accelerate to a higher level of purity, an ever more pure expression of wisdom. I am the spirit of the Second Ray. I AM Lanto!

11 | I INVOKE A PURE MOTIVE FOR SEEKING WISDOM

In the name I AM THAT I AM, Jesus Christ, I call to my I AM Presence to flow through the I Will Be Presence that I AM and give this invocation with full power. I call to beloved Elohim Apollo and Lumina and Purity and Astrea, Archangel Jophiel and Christine and Gabriel and Hope, Master Lanto and Serapis Bey to help me transcend all ego-based motivation for seeking wisdom and using it to force or impress others. Help me see and surrender all patterns that block my oneness with Master Lanto and my oneness with my I AM Presence, including …

[Make personal calls]

1. I find ever-changing security

1. Master Lanto, help me attain clarity about my intentions for using wisdom. Help me see through and surrender the ego's quest for security and its desire to find an infallible form of wisdom.

Beloved Apollo, with your second ray,
you open my eyes to see a new day,
I see through duality's lies and deceit,
transcending the mindset producing defeat.

**Beloved Apollo, thou Elohim Gold,
your radiant light my eyes now behold,
as pages of wisdom you gently unfold,
I feel I am free from all that is old.**

2. Master Lanto, help me see the ego-based tendency to claim that I have the highest possible motives for my use of wisdom, and that it is in the interest of other people, and in the interest of some higher cause, that I seek to force my wisdom upon others.

Beloved Apollo, in your flame I know,
that your living wisdom is always a flow,
in your light I see my own highest will,
immersed in the stream that never stands still.

**Beloved Apollo, your light makes it clear,
why we have taken embodiment here,
working to raise our own cosmic sphere,
together we form the tip of the spear.**

3. Master Lanto, help me see that the ego's so-called absolute wisdom is entirely relative. It is completely relative to what my ego has accepted and to the sense of security that the ego has built.

11 | I Invoke a Pure Motive for Seeking Wisdom

> Beloved Apollo, exposing all lies,
> I hereby surrender all ego-based ties,
> I know my perception is truly the key,
> to transcending the serpentine duality.
>
> **Beloved Apollo, we heed now your call,**
> **drawing us into Wisdom's Great Hall,**
> **exposing all lies causing the fall,**
> **you help us reclaim the oneness of all.**

4. Master Lanto, help me, as the Conscious You, experience pure awareness and realize that my own nature is an absolute state of security—not in the sense that it is unchanging, but in the sense that it is ever-transcending.

> Beloved Apollo, your wisdom so clear,
> in oneness with you, no serpent I fear,
> the beam in my eye I'm willing to see,
> I'm free from the serpent's own duality.
>
> **Beloved Apollo, my eyes now I raise,**
> **I see that the Earth is in a new phase,**
> **I willingly stand in your piercing gaze,**
> **empowered, I exit duality's maze.**

5. Master Lanto, help me experience that at the core of my being is that which is unchanging, namely awareness. I am connecting to that unchanging awareness. I am finding security in constantly transcending the outer expressions of awareness.

> Beloved Astrea, your heart is so true,
> your Circle and Sword of white and blue,
> cut all life free from dramas unwise,
> on wings of Purity our planet will rise.

**Beloved Astrea, in God Purity,
accelerate all of my life energy,
raising my mind into true unity
with the Masters of love in Infinity.**

6. I do *not* need to stop the flow of the River of Life in order to feel secure; I feel secure in flowing with it. This is absolute or ultimate security, but it is security through self-transcendence. It is the security that is ever-flowing.

Beloved Astrea, from Purity's Ray,
send forth deliverance to all life today,
acceleration to Purity, I AM now free
from all that is less than love's Purity.

**Beloved Astrea, in oneness with you,
your circle and sword of electric blue,
with Purity's Light cutting right through,
raising within me all that is true.**

7. Master Lanto, help me see that the harder I try to maintain the outer security of my ego, the more I will generate energy impulses that are sent into the cosmic mirror. These energy impulses will be returned as conditions that seek to threaten the ego's sense of security.

Beloved Astrea, accelerate us all,
as for your deliverance I fervently call,
set all life free from vision impure
beyond fear and doubt, I AM rising for sure.

**Beloved Astrea, I AM willing to see,
all of the lies that keep me unfree,
I AM rising beyond every impurity,
with Purity's Light forever in me.**

8. I must, therefore, send more powerful impulses to counteract this return, and this generates an even stronger return. Master Lanto, help me see the fallacy of this before I break under the strain.

Beloved Astrea, accelerate life
beyond all duality's struggle and strife,
consume all division between God and man,
accelerate fulfillment of God's perfect plan.

**Beloved Astrea, I lovingly call,
break down separation's invisible wall,
I surrender all lies causing the fall,
forever affirming the oneness of All.**

9. Master Lanto, I hereby surrender all tendency to use wisdom as a kind of force in order to build the security of my ego.

Accelerate my Awakeness, I AM real,
Accelerate my Awakeness, all life heal,
Accelerate my Awakeness, I AM MORE,
Accelerate my Awakeness, all will soar.

Accelerate my Awakeness! (3X)
Beloved Apollo and Lumina.
Accelerate my Awakeness! (3X)
Beloved Jophiel and Christine.
Accelerate my Awakeness! (3X)
Beloved Master Lanto.
Accelerate my Awakeness! (3X)
Beloved I AM.

2. I am open to the flow of the spirit

1. Acceleration means that I go beyond accumulating power at a certain level. I am accelerating my vibration to a higher level where I am no longer feeling the lower energies when they are returned to me by the cosmic mirror.

Jophiel Archangel, in wisdom's great light,
all serpentine lies exposed to my sight.
So subtle the lies that creep through the mind,
yet you are the greatest teacher I find.

Jophiel Archangel, exposing all lies,
Jophiel Archangel, cutting all ties.
Jophiel Archangel, clearing the skies,
Jophiel Archangel, my mind truly flies.

2. The lower energies pass right through me. They are insignificant to me. They are irrelevant to my life experience. This is true acceleration, and in this there is security because I am transcending the past.

> Jophiel Archangel, your wisdom I hail,
> your sword cutting through duality's veil.
> As you show the way, I know what is real,
> from serpentine doubt, I instantly heal.
>
> **Jophiel Archangel, exposing all lies,**
> **Jophiel Archangel, cutting all ties.**
> **Jophiel Archangel, clearing the skies,**
> **Jophiel Archangel, my mind truly flies.**

3. Master Lanto, help me see that the wisdom, the thought systems, created by the ego are truly relative, even though they claim to be absolute. They are relative because they are relative to the duality consciousness, and they have an opposite.

> Jophiel Archangel, your reality,
> the best antidote to duality.
> No lie can remain in your Presence so clear,
> with you on my side, no serpent I fear.
>
> **Jophiel Archangel, exposing all lies,**
> **Jophiel Archangel, cutting all ties.**
> **Jophiel Archangel, clearing the skies,**
> **Jophiel Archangel, my mind truly flies.**

4. Something that is relative is not absolute wisdom. Master Lanto, help me experience pure awareness until I experience that I can find this inner security instead of the outer security of an absolute or infallible belief system.

> Jophiel Archangel, God's mind is in me,
> and through your clear light, its wisdom I see.
> Divisions all vanish, as I see the One,
> and truly, the wholeness of mind I have won.

**Jophiel Archangel, exposing all lies,
Jophiel Archangel, cutting all ties.
Jophiel Archangel, clearing the skies,
Jophiel Archangel, my mind truly flies.**

5. Master Lanto, help me have a direct experience of the spirit of the Chohan of the Second Ray. I am opening my mind so that the Spirit of the Second Ray is streaming through my mind. I am experiencing that spirit, as the spirit is being expressed through me.

Gabriel Archangel, your light I revere,
immersed in your Presence, nothing I fear.
A disciple of Christ, I do leave behind,
the ego's desire for responding in kind.

**Gabriel Archangel, of this I am sure,
Gabriel Archangel, Christ light is the cure.
Gabriel Archangel, intentions so pure,
Gabriel Archangel, in you I'm secure.**

6. Master Lanto, I am using your description as a stepping stone for opening my mind to the direct experience. I am surrendering my ego's attachment to a particular worded expression of wisdom. An expression of wisdom is only a description, and it has value only if I use it to open my mind to a direct experience of the spirit behind the words.

Gabriel Archangel, I fear not the light,
in purifications' fire, I delight.
With your hand in mine, each challenge I face,
I follow the spiral to infinite grace.

**Gabriel Archangel, of this I am sure,
Gabriel Archangel, Christ light is the cure.
Gabriel Archangel, intentions so pure,
Gabriel Archangel, in you I'm secure.**

7. God is not static. God is the ever-flowing, ever-transcending spirit. I am surrendering the sense of distance between myself and the spirit. I am coming into gnosis with the spirit, I am becoming an open door so that the spirit flows through me.

Gabriel Archangel, your fire burning white,
ascending with you, out of the night.
My ego has nowhere to run and to hide,
in ascension's bright spiral, with you I abide.

**Gabriel Archangel, of this I am sure,
Gabriel Archangel, Christ light is the cure.
Gabriel Archangel, intentions so pure,
Gabriel Archangel, in you I'm secure.**

8. I am allowing the spirit to flow through me by surrendering any tendency to demand that the spirit conform to or validate any expression on earth. I surrender any tendency to impose a restriction on the spirit. I am allowing the spirit to flow freely.

Gabriel Archangel, your trumpet I hear,
announcing the birth of Christ drawing near.
In lightness of being, I now am reborn,
rising with Christ on bright Easter morn.

**Gabriel Archangel, of this I am sure,
Gabriel Archangel, Christ light is the cure.
Gabriel Archangel, intentions so pure,
Gabriel Archangel, in you I'm secure.**

9. Master Lanto, I am following your words to their source. I am experiencing your spirit and accelerating myself beyond the level of duality.

> With angels I soar,
> as I reach for MORE.
> The angels so real,
> their love all will heal.
> The angels bring peace,
> all conflicts will cease.
> With angels of light,
> we soar to new height.
>
> **The rustling sound of angel wings,**
> **what joy as even matter sings,**
> **what joy as every atom rings,**
> **in harmony with angel wings.**

3. I am raising my motivation for seeking wisdom

1. Master Lanto, help me pass the initiation of realizing what the path of initiation is all about. At every step, my task is to take the very next step, to pass the very next initiation. I am willing to acquire the wisdom that challenges my current mental box so that I can accelerate myself beyond it.

> Master Lanto, golden wise,
> expose in me the ego's lies.
> Master Lanto, will to be,
> I will to win my mastery.

11 | I Invoke a Pure Motive for Seeking Wisdom

O Holy Spirit, flow through me,
I am the open door for thee.
O mighty rushing stream of Light,
transcendence is my sacred right.

2. The highest wisdom is always the wisdom that I can grasp with my present level of consciousness but that can still accelerate me to the next level up. This wisdom is relative to both the level of consciousness where I am at and the level that is immediately above.

Master Lanto, balance all,
for wisdom's balance I do call.
Master Lanto, help me see,
that balance is the Golden key.

O Holy Spirit, flow through me,
I am the open door for thee.
O mighty rushing stream of Light,
transcendence is my sacred right.

3. I surrender the ego-based desire for acquiring some ultimate form of wisdom and then going out and impressing other people with my superior wisdom.

Master Lanto, from Above,
I call forth discerning love.
Master Lanto, love's not blind,
through love, God vision I will find.

O Holy Spirit, flow through me,
I am the open door for thee.
O mighty rushing stream of Light,
transcendence is my sacred right.

4. I am stopping my conscious mind from going into a fear mode. I will accept the ideas that can take me to the next level of consciousness.

> Master Lanto, pure I am,
> intentions pure as Christic lamb.
> Master Lanto, I will transcend,
> acceleration now my truest friend.
>
> **O Holy Spirit, flow through me,**
> **I am the open door for thee.**
> **O mighty rushing stream of Light,**
> **transcendence is my sacred right.**

5. I surrender the desire to find the ultimate teaching, and thereby I transcend the fear of having a false teaching. I will *not* be so afraid of accepting false ideas that I dare not consider true ideas. I will *not* be so afraid of the false hierarchy that I close my mind to the true teachers of the ascended masters.

> Master Lanto, I am whole,
> no more division in my soul.
> Master Lanto, healing flame,
> all balance in your sacred name.
>
> **O Holy Spirit, flow through me,**
> **I am the open door for thee.**
> **O mighty rushing stream of Light,**
> **transcendence is my sacred right.**

6. My intention for acquiring wisdom is to transcend my present level of consciousness. I can do this in only one way, namely by making direct contact with spiritual teachers who are beyond my present level.

11 | I Invoke a Pure Motive for Seeking Wisdom

Master Lanto, serve all life,
as I transcend all inner strife.
Master Lanto, peace you give,
to all who want to truly live.

**O Holy Spirit, flow through me,
I am the open door for thee.
O mighty rushing stream of Light,
transcendence is my sacred right.**

7. I surrender the desire to seek a form of magic that will give me automatic mastery, the false mastery of those who seek to take heaven by force. I am willing to let my ego-based self die. I am willing to look at the beam in my own eye, I am willing to give up the ego.

Master Lanto, free to be,
in balanced creativity.
Master Lanto, we employ,
your balance as the key to joy.

**O Holy Spirit, flow through me,
I am the open door for thee.
O mighty rushing stream of Light,
transcendence is my sacred right.**

8. I am a true student. I want to raise up myself first of all, but I also want to raise up all life. I am raising my intention, and I am seeking wisdom in order to accelerate myself to the next level of consciousness.

> Master Lanto, balance all,
> the seven rays upon my call.
> Master Lanto, I take flight,
> my threefold flame a blazing light.

> **O Holy Spirit, flow through me,**
> **I am the open door for thee.**
> **O mighty rushing stream of Light,**
> **transcendence is my sacred right.**

9. I am seeking to acquire a wisdom that is useful for inspiring others. I look at people openly and honestly and consider where they are in consciousness. I seek to give them something that will take them one step higher.

> Lanto dear, your Presence here,
> filling up my inner sphere.
> Life is now a sacred flow,
> God Wisdom I on all bestow.

> **O Holy Spirit, flow through me,**
> **I am the open door for thee.**
> **O mighty rushing stream of Light,**
> **transcendence is my sacred right.**

4. There are no failures on the path

1. I hereby make the conscious choice that I want the spirit more than anything else. By accelerating my intention and by being willing to continually accelerate my intention, I am accelerating myself away from the false hierarchy impostors and their false teaching.

Serapis Bey, what power lies,
behind your purifying eyes.
Serapis Bey, it is a treat,
to enter your sublime retreat.

**O Holy Spirit, flow through me,
I am the open door for thee.
O mighty rushing stream of Light,
transcendence is my sacred right.**

2. What does it matter if I have accepted a false teaching when I am continually accelerating myself? I will come to see that it was false, and in seeing that it was false, I have accelerated myself and acquired discernment.

Serapis Bey, what wisdom found,
your words are always most profound.
Serapis Bey, I tell you true,
my mind has room for naught but you.

**O Holy Spirit, flow through me,
I am the open door for thee.
O mighty rushing stream of Light,
transcendence is my sacred right.**

3. The process of the ascension is that I discover one thousand ways *not* to make an ascended master. For each way I discover *not* to make an ascended master, I take one step up. Finally, I will be at the step where I can discover the *one* way to *make* an ascended master—and then, I *am* an ascended master.

Serapis Bey, what love beyond,
my heart does leap, as I respond.
Serapis Bey, your life a poem,
that calls me to my starry home.

**O Holy Spirit, flow through me,
I am the open door for thee.
O mighty rushing stream of Light,
transcendence is my sacred right.**

4. There is no such thing as a failed experiment on the path of the ascension. Whether it works or it doesn't work, I will learn from it and accelerate myself to a higher level of consciousness.

Serapis Bey, your guidance sure,
my base is clear and white and pure.
Serapis Bey, no longer trapped,
by soul in which my self was wrapped.

**O Holy Spirit, flow through me,
I am the open door for thee.
O mighty rushing stream of Light,
transcendence is my sacred right.**

5. Master Lanto, I recognize that you are the Chohan of the Second Ray because *you are one* with the spirit of the Second Ray.

Serapis Bey, what healing balm,
in mind that is forever calm.
Serapis Bey, my thoughts are pure,
your discipline I shall endure.

11 | I Invoke a Pure Motive for Seeking Wisdom

O Holy Spirit, flow through me,
I am the open door for thee.
O mighty rushing stream of Light,
transcendence is my sacred right.

6. Master Lanto, I recognize that *you are* the Second Ray. You have risen to a level where you no longer see yourself as being one with the Second Ray, for *you are* the Second Ray!

Serapis Bey, what secret test,
for egos who want to be best.
Serapis Bey, expose in me,
all that is less than harmony.

O Holy Spirit, flow through me,
I am the open door for thee.
O mighty rushing stream of Light,
transcendence is my sacred right.

7. Master Lanto, I recognize that you are the representative of the Second Ray for earth. There is none other. There is no spirit that is flowing through you.

Serapis Bey, what moving sight,
my self ascends to sacred height.
Serapis Bey, forever free,
in sacred synchronicity.

O Holy Spirit, flow through me,
I am the open door for thee.
O mighty rushing stream of Light,
transcendence is my sacred right.

8. Master Lanto, I recognize that *you are* the spirit that is flowing, and I am willing to have your spirit flow through me. I am opening myself up to the flow that will help me transcend my current level by challenging my current mental box.

> Serapis Bey, you balance all,
> the seven rays upon my call.
> Serapis Bey, in space and time,
> the pyramid of self, I climb.

> **O Holy Spirit, flow through me,**
> **I am the open door for thee.**
> **O mighty rushing stream of Light,**
> **transcendence is my sacred right.**

9. Master Lanto, I am willing to be challenged, and you are willing to challenge. We will both flow to a higher level, we can accelerate to a higher level of purity, an ever more pure expression of wisdom. I am one with the spirit of the Second Ray that *is* Lanto!

> Serapis Bey, your Presence here,
> filling up my inner sphere.
> Life is now a sacred flow,
> God Purity I do bestow.

> **O Holy Spirit, flow through me,**
> **I am the open door for thee.**
> **O mighty rushing stream of Light,**
> **transcendence is my sacred right.**

Sealing:

In the name of the Divine Mother, I fully accept that the power of these calls is used to set free the Ma-ter light, so it can outpicture the perfect vision of Christ for my own life, for all people and for the planet. In the name I AM THAT I AM, it is done! Amen.

12 | WISDOM AND VISION

I AM the Ascended Master Lanto! I come to discourse on the initiations that you go through when you come to the fifth level of initiations in the Royal Teton Retreat. This is, of course, the level of the Fifth Ray, which has often been called the ray of truth, the ray of healing or the ray of vision. What I would like to make you aware of here is that there is an element of the Fifth Ray that has generally not been known, even by students of the ascended masters.

The Third Eye Chakra

The Fifth Ray is, of course, related to the so-called Third Eye Chakra in the center of the brow. It is said that when this chakra is activated, you gain the ability to see things that you cannot see with the physical sight. Many spiritual people have heard stories of those who have had their third eye opened and can now see auras or other phenomena. Many think this is highly desirable and it is a sign of spiritual attainment. In reality, it may not be the sign of spiritual attainment at all, as you will clearly see in many of the so-called psychics you find in the world. They may have some ability to tune in to something beyond the material realm, but they often do not have the spiritual maturity to know how to deal with this.

There is an element of the Fifth Ray, of spiritual vision, that is not generally known. You will, of course, know from yourselves and your own experience how many people in the world are very attached to the concept of truth. I have spoken about this before, of how people think there is one particular expression of wisdom, one particular thought system or belief system, that is the superior truth or the superior wisdom. Many ascended masters' students are so attached to one particular outer teaching that they cannot even follow us as we move on with the delivery of the Living Word that is an ongoing flow that will not stop until the last person has ascended from earth.

The dream of a secret formula

When people come to the fifth level of initiation in my retreat, they often think that now it is a matter of them going into our library and discovering a secret book that contains a secret formula that will suddenly give them these superhuman abilities. Just look at how many people in the world are chasing the pot of gold at the end of the rainbow. Some people are literally chasing a physical pot of gold in the form of material riches, but look at how many spiritual students are chasing a metaphorical pot of gold by seeking to acquire some kind of knowledge, or formula, or ability that is beyond the normal. This is a great hindrance for students on the spiritual path, and you need to shed it at some point or another and why not right here in my retreat at the Royal Teton?

We are fully capable of helping you acquire the wisdom that will allow you to dismiss this ego-based chase for superhuman abilities. What have I said about the ego? It seeks ultimate security. If you suddenly had some kind of secret formula or some kind of superhuman ability, would that not give you and your ego a sense of security? Yet, if you were to acquire this ability and if it would give your ego a sense of security, then would that actually further your spiritual progress? On the contrary, it would hinder your spiritual progress and put you in a blind alley.

We have many students who come to our retreat being in such a blind alley where they either have acquired some knowledge or some ability or where they dream of acquiring it. They come, thinking that we should help them acquire some superhuman ability. They also come, of course, thinking that truth can be expressed in words and that it must be possible to find some worded statement that is an absolute truth. We have a library at the Royal Teton Retreat that contains all of the spiritual teachings ever brought forth on earth. It is a parallel to the famous Library of Alexandria but far more extensive. Our library goes all the way back to previous civilizations long forgotten. You know of Atlantis and Lemuria, but our library goes back to civilizations that have never even been named.

When people have this quest for truth, for ultimate truth given in words, we put them into that library and we say: "Spend as much time as you like here searching for this truth, and let us know when you have found something." They eagerly throw themselves at this library. At first, they are enormously excited and almost overwhelmed by the amount of books in the library, for there truly are millions of volumes. They pick some and they start reading. They become very excited, thinking they have found a very high expression of truth.

Then, they find another book that also has seemingly great authority and great depth and great wisdom, and they now read this. They go on and read another, and it is just a matter of how long it takes before they start realizing that there are many different expressions of truth that all seem valid, that all seem to have authority, but they are all a little bit different, or in some cases very different.

This leads students to a point of frustration where they don't know what to believe. You will recognize this, perhaps, from your own life or at least from many people in the world who have become agnostics as a result of the unresolved war between science and religion. They don't know what to believe, or they believe that there is no ultimate truth. Am I hereby saying that we want ascended master students to become agnostics? Not in a worldly sense, but we do want you to come to the point where you realize, as I have mentioned before, that no statement made with words can be an ultimate truth.

What you see with an open third eye

This is an absolutely necessary realization on the path. What do you then do? When a student comes to this point of frustration, then we can step in and help them. Why do we allow them to come to this point of frustration? Because when they come to our retreat being fully convinced that there must be an absolute truth, they are not open to hearing us tell them that this is not the case. They need to experience the frustration before they open their minds to what we will give them next.

What we do next is that we take them into a special room where we can display on a screen what you can actually see if you have your third eye opened to the highest possible degree. There are a variety of psychics in the world who have their third eyes opened to a lesser or greater degree. However, very few people in embodiment have had their third eye opened to the ultimate degree.

What we show students on a screen is what you see if you have your third eye opened to the full extent. We show students that when you take a statement made by words, those words are not actually physical words. As you know from science, there is no such thing as physical matter. Matter is simply a more dense form of energy, which is why you can perceive it with the physical senses. When you are able to see with an opened third eye, you can see the energy behind matter, you can see the flow of energy behind outer forms. We can now take any statement made by words and run it through a special apparatus, somewhat similar to a computer but far more advanced, and then we can display on the screen the energy produced by the words.

If you want a visual illustration, consider the computer programs that you can use for recording and editing sound. The sound is stored as bits of zeros and ones on the computer's drive, but on the screen, they are displayed as waves or lines that go up and down. You can now play the sound and see the waves. You can change various things and change the waves. This is somewhat similar (although far more primitive) to what we have at the Royal Teton Retreat. We can show students that when you take a certain statement of words and run it through the device, then there is a display on the screen of the energy flow created by the words.

We can show a student whether this energy flow goes upwards or downwards or whether it simply stands still in one place. We can then show them that there is a variety of the spiritual, political, scientific or religious teachings found on earth that actually create a downwards energetic flow. If you read those words and take them into your mind, or if they are read aloud on radio and television, those that hear them actually experience a downwards flow in their energy fields.

We can also show how the vast majority of the music, of the words, the newscasts, that are broadcast on radio, television or over the Internet, produce energy waves that simply tread water, so to speak. They move up and down, but they do not really have a decisive movement in an upwards or downwards direction. They just stand still and move in place. We can also show that there are some statements with words that produce an upwards energy flow. These are, of course, the statements that will raise your consciousness. Yet here comes the interesting part. Any statement expressed with words in the material universe can only produce an energy impulse that goes so far.

Dictations have a particular goal

If you are at a certain level of consciousness right now and you hear or read this dictation, this particular dictation, it is likely that the dictation will raise your level of consciousness. It creates an upwards impulse, an upwards energetic impulse, that will raise your state of consciousness—if you tune in to it and if you allow yourself to be raised up. It is, of course, perfectly possible to read or hear this dictation and either not tune in to it or refuse to be raised above your present level of consciousness. For those who are willing, the dictation can take them higher than their present level, unless of course they are already higher than the level of consciousness for which this dictation is given.

What we can show is that any statement expressed in words is given for a certain level of consciousness. Any statement is given for one of the 144 possible levels of consciousness found on earth. The purpose of this particular dictation is to reach those who are at the fifth level of initiation under the Second Ray and then give you an energy impulse that can take you to the sixth level. This statement is not given for the 144th level, and it is not meant to be an ultimate truth. It is not meant to take you from your current level to the 144th level. It is only meant to take you one level up, and this it will do.

What happens if you were to think that this dictation was an ultimate statement of truth? What we can make visible on the screen is that the energy flow created by this dictation will take you up to a certain level, but then it will begin to circle around. From now on, you will only stay at that level. Because the energy flows around in a circle, there will be a certain sense of up and down. If you look at a circle, when the energy flows down one side, you have a sense of going down. When it flows up the other side, you have a sense of going up.

This is important because it shows you what happens to many spiritual students when they find a particular teaching. As I said, this dictation is meant to take you one level up. There are many spiritual teachings in the world that are directed at several levels of consciousness, and they can take you a number of levels up. Any teaching in the world has a limited range. It cannot be any other way. You cannot give a teaching for the 144th level that will appeal to somebody at the 10th level. They will have no way of even grasping the teaching.

A teaching can only have a range, which means that even if a teaching takes you up several levels of consciousness, there *will* come a point where you do not go higher. Now, the teaching begins to be like a wave in the ocean that moves around in a circle. This means that there will be points where you are going down in consciousness even though you are still following the teaching. You may not notice that you are going down, but then there comes a point where the energy starts flowing back up and now you feel like you are going up. If you notice you are going up, you think the teaching is still helping you grow. This is why it is possible for students to remain with a certain outer teaching for years, for decades, even for lifetimes, before they have had enough of it and realize they need to find something that can take them to the next level.

This is a very important mechanism for you to understand with the outer, conscious mind because it can prevent you from getting into the blind alley that many, many spiritual students have gotten into by thinking they had to remain loyal to an outer teaching, outer guru or outer organization. When students see this, when they truly grasp this, it is as if a great burden has been lifted from them. They now see that they can let go of a certain teaching, guru or organization without any negative reaction.

When students realize there is no ultimate teaching

What happens to many students in the world is that they find a certain teaching. For some time, they are very enthusiastic about it, thinking that it will give them the ultimate security that their egos crave. They think they have found the pot of gold at the end of the rainbow by finding this teaching, guru or organization. They think they only have to stay in it and continue doing the same thing, and then one day they will ascend, reach Nirvana or whatever the goal is.

After some time, they reach that point from which they cannot go higher with the teaching and now they begin to go in circles. For some of the more perceptive students, there can come a point where they realize they are going in circles, they realize they are not going anywhere. If they do not understand that the teaching was never meant to take them any higher, then they might become resentful and angry. They might feel that the guru or the teaching has made empty promises. In some cases, a guru *will* have made empty promises. In other cases, it is simply the students' egos that have caused them to interpret the teaching as being this empty promise, but the promise was not empty. It was simply the interpretation that made it false, for the ego is, of course, always looking for the easy way out, the guaranteed, automatic salvation.

What happens to many of these students? Deep within, beyond the conscious level of the mind, they know they have to move on from the teaching. If their outer minds are still attached to the teaching or the promises made by the teaching, then, in many cases, the only way they can break free is that they suddenly snap out of their sense that the teaching must be ultimate. They realize this is false, and now they become angry and accuse the guru or the teaching of making a false promise.

The problem with this reaction is that it will take the students back down the staircase formed by the levels of consciousness. There are many, many students who have found a teaching, who have used it to raise themselves up several levels, and then, by becoming angry, they go down several levels, sometimes even further down than they were taken up by the teaching. Many have gotten themselves into a blind alley. Many have become almost like agnostics, thinking that there is no teaching that works, there is no guru who is true. If you can understand what I am saying here, if you can lock in to this with the conscious mind, then you can realize that a teaching is only meant to take you a certain level up.

When it has done so, it is time to tune in to this. It is, in fact, your responsibility to tune in to this, and then you need to make the decision to move on. When the student is ready, the teacher appears. When you are willing to let go of an existing teaching and open your mind to the inner direction from your Christ self and your ascended teachers, you *will* receive it. If you are attuning your outer mind, you will know with your outer mind that you have received it. You will be able to move on without going into a negative reaction, without feeling like you are in a vacuum. In order to get to that point, you must let go.

Seeing the hooks in your consciousness

We can show students on the screen a picture of their own energy fields. We put them in front of a scanner, and then we display on the screen where they have certain hooks in their consciousness that tie them to a particular teaching on earth. This is what makes them a house divided against themselves. It pulls them in different directions or it pulls them back down the staircase. There is something they haven't let go of, and they cannot move with the River of Life because it is like their boat has an anchor that keeps it in place or keeps it going in the wrong direction. Or it keeps it almost in the wrong angle compared to the current of the river so that there is turmoil and brushing of waters. When students begin to see this and cut the tie, they see how free they are. The tricky part of this is that you are not truly free until you also see with the conscious mind and make the conscious decision to cut the tie. What we *can do* at the Royal Teton Retreat is to help you see the ties that you have and cut them at the level of the identity, mental and emotional bodies. What we *cannot do* at the retreat is to help you cut them at the level of the conscious mind. This is what *you* must do consciously from your normal, waking awareness. This is, of course, much easier to do when the work has been done from the three higher levels, but it still requires a conscious awareness, a conscious effort and a conscious decision.

When you do cut these ties consciously, you will feel a new sense of freedom, a new sense of being healed of old wounds and conflicts. Your ego and the false teachers do not want you to cut these ties. That is why they will try to make you feel like you to have to remain loyal, like you have to close your conscious mind to the insights you already gained at higher levels of the mind. They are desperately seeking to make you cling to what you have without moving on.

Until you move on, you cannot actually be healed. Until you are healed from the divisions that pull your mind in different directions, how can you attain the higher vision that is the hallmark of the Fifth Ray? If you do not attain this vision, how can you feel whole? If you do not feel whole, how can you be the open door for the healing of others? "Physician, heal thyself," as the old saying goes. What we can show people is how to use wisdom to heal your wounds, how to use wisdom to heal others by reasoning with others and by reasoning with yourself.

Use dictations to grow consciously

What is the purpose of this dictation and the other dictations given by me and the other Chohans? It is to give you tools for reasoning with yourself at the level of the conscious mind. When you study a dictation, two things will happen. You will receive spiritual light, and this light begins to create a transformation in your energy field.

You will also receive outer knowledge in the form of words. The question is what you do with those words. Some students simply read them and say: "Oh yes! That was interesting." Others study them more intently, and some even learn certain statements by heart, thinking, that if they memorize the statements, they must have learned the lesson. One of the lessons that we desire you to learn is that you read a dictation until you come to certain statements that do one of two things. They either stir something in you so you feel you have touched the hem of the garment of a higher reality, or they stir a reaction in you where you feel a resistance to the statement. When you feel this resistance, this is when you have the opportunity to use the teaching to start reasoning with yourself. You can, with your conscious mind, begin to explore what the resistance is.

You understand, of course, that a book like this must make general statements. I cannot personally address every student that might read this book in the future. It is *your* job to take the book and relate it to your personal situation. When you feel a resistance or an unresolved question concerning a statement made in the book, then it is *your* responsibility to explore what the resistance means. You ask yourself questions. You try to tune in. You try to go around and say: "But what if the statement was true? What would that mean? How would that help me be free? What is the fear that I feel concerning this statement? What is the doubt? What are the questions that come up in my mind?"

Then, you explore them and you try to go around them, and you try to go deeper and deeper. You are reasoning with yourself in order to clarify which aspect of your ego, which of the spirits in your consciousness, opposes this statement. By doing this, you can expose the spirit, but you can expose also the belief that created that spirit, the particular dualistic illusion that created the spirit. When you do this, you can come to that point, as we have talked about, where you see, you experience, the illusion. In experiencing it, you spontaneously, you instantly, you effortlessly let it go.

This is *your* responsibility as a student of the ascended masters. You cannot expect that reading a book is enough. You cannot even expect that just practicing the invocations is enough. Certainly, they have an effect, but nothing can work against your free will. There must come that point where you consciously and deliberately look at the beam, the spirit, in your own eye. You look at the illusions. You keep looking at them from different angles, probing them with different questions, until you see the very core belief behind the illusion. When you see it in the light of Christ truth, you see that it is unreal, that it is an illusion. At that moment, you have no trouble letting it go.

Be healed by giving up illusions of being unwhole

This is also an element of the Fifth Ray of healing. What does it take to be healed? You must let go of the state of being unhealed. If you do not let go of the sense that you are not healed, you cannot enter the state of mind where you are healed, where you are whole. You cannot let go of the disease or the illusion until you see it as unreal. You cannot see this without seeing it through the Christ mind, but you will not automatically gain the Christ vision. You will gain it only by systematically and consciously challenging the illusions, going towards deeper levels until you find the belief that you personally accepted sometime in the past, and it is now an anchor, holding your boat back and preventing it from flowing with the River of Life.

This is what in Buddhism is called the Prajna boat, the boat of wisdom, where you get into it and you can navigate the sea of Samsara until you reach the farther shore. The farther shore is in Buddhism often seen as some ultimate state, Nirvana. But the farther shore at your particular level of consciousness is when you pass the initiation that takes you to the next level up. There is more than one "farther shore." The farther shore is the next shore, the next level up, and you keep going towards the next level until you reach the 144th and then take that last quantum leap into the ascended state.

Wholeness comes from giving up the sense of being unwhole, and a very big step towards this is to give up the dream of finding some ultimate truth or ultimate formula or gaining some ultimate ability. Nothing in the material world is ultimate. Nothing is finite. Nothing is the end. Everything is the River of Life that constantly flows on. If you could truly integrate this truth, you would make it so much easier for yourself to walk the path of initiation under the seven rays. Instead of feeling like you are a constant failure because you have not attained the ultimate state, you could feel that you are going from one victory to another every time you pass another initiation.

The ascended masters do not judge you

We have seen ascended master students who have been in an ascended master teaching for 30 or 40 years or even more. They have been diligent in studying the teaching. They have been diligent in invoking the violet flame or giving other decrees for the other rays. They have done everything right in the outer sense, but their entire path has been a struggle. They have heard and accepted the teaching of the path of initiation, but they have still focused their minds on the end goal, whether it was the ascension or something else. They have been so focused on attaining this end goal that they have felt that until they attain it, they will be inadequate, they are not good enough, they are not acceptable to the ascended masters.

We do not judge you the way you judge yourself. I AM Lanto; I AM the Chohan of the Second Ray. It is *not* my role to take you to the ultimate level of initiation. It is my role to take you from one level to the next through the seven levels represented by the Second Ray initiations and then hand you off to my beloved brother, Paul the Venetian, who will take you through the Third Ray initiations.

Do you really think that I, Lanto, look at you as an inadequate student? The entire time you are going through the initiations in my retreat, I look at you in a positive light. I look at you as a student who has attained the victory of passing through the seven initiations under Master MORE and the First Ray. I look at you as having won an important victory before you even enter my retreat, and then, when you pass the first level of initiation, you win another important victory and so on. When you get to the final initiation in my retreat, you win what I consider the highest victory at my level of initiation, and I am gratified that I can send you on to the next level up.

Where is the defeat? Where is the inadequacy? You are the perfect student when you arrive, not that you are perfect, not that you have attained the highest level of consciousness, but you have passed the initiations of the First Ray before you arrive at my retreat. How is that not a victory? How can you feel inadequate when you have gone through the difficult and rigorous initiations under the First Ray? Master MORE will not send you to me until you have passed the initiations and *that,* I can assure you, is a victory. I will not send you to Paul the Venetian until you have passed the initiations under the Second Ray, and *that* is another victory.

Stop chasing the remote pot of gold at the end of the rainbow, for I tell you, as Maitreya has said in his book, not only is there no pot of gold, but there is no rainbow. The rainbow keeps moving in front of you, just like the carrot dangling in front of the nose of the proverbial donkey. You will never catch up. You will never catch up to the rainbow, my beloved, for the rainbow exists only from a certain viewpoint. It has no fixed or objective existence. It is relative to your viewpoint, and you will always see the rainbow at a distance. If you get close, you can no longer see it so how do you know where it ends?

Give up the quest for ultimate truth. Realize that any statement made with words can take you only so much higher, and then you need to open yourself up to receiving the next teaching, the next statement, the next clue, the next experience. Be willing to experience the Spirit of Truth beyond the outer statement of truth. This is the hallmark of the students who make swift progress and who pass the fifth level of initiation on the Second Ray.

I AM the Chohan of the Second Ray. I will do everything I can to help you pass that initiation, but *I cannot pass it for you* because it requires a decision with the conscious mind. Before you can make that spontaneous decision, you must be willing to reason with yourself and probe why your ego has this quest for ultimate truth. What is the particular belief that you have personally accepted and that makes you vulnerable to this impossible quest, thinking there must be some way to find some ultimate truth or some ultimate ability? Let go of it, my beloved, and then you can step up to the sixth level of initiation under the Second Ray. I am ready and willing to welcome you to that level of initiation. Lanto I AM.

13 | I INVOKE AN ATTITUDE OF ONGOING VICTORY

In the name I AM THAT I AM, Jesus Christ, I call to my I AM Presence to flow through the I Will Be Presence that I AM and give this invocation with full power. I call to beloved Elohim Apollo and Lumina and Cyclopea and Virginia, Archangel Jophiel and Christine and Raphael and Mother Mary, Master Lanto and Hilarion to help me overcome all sense of being inadequate so I can adopt a sense that the path goes from one victory to the next. Help me see and surrender all patterns that block my oneness with Master Lanto and my oneness with my I AM Presence, including …

[Make personal calls]

1. I am loyal to the inner path

1. Master Lanto, help me acquire the wisdom that will allow me to dismiss the ego-based chase for superhuman abilities. I surrender the desire to have my third eye opened or be able to heal others.

Beloved Apollo, with your second ray,
you open my eyes to see a new day,
I see through duality's lies and deceit,
transcending the mindset producing defeat.

**Beloved Apollo, thou Elohim Gold,
your radiant light my eyes now behold,
as pages of wisdom you gently unfold,
I feel I am free from all that is old.**

2. Master Lanto, help me develop my heart's ability to discern whether the energy behind any physical phenomenon flows upwards or downwards or whether it simply stands still in one place.

Beloved Apollo, in your flame I know,
that your living wisdom is always a flow,
in your light I see my own highest will,
immersed in the stream that never stands still.

**Beloved Apollo, your light makes it clear,
why we have taken embodiment here,
working to raise our own cosmic sphere,
together we form the tip of the spear.**

3. Master Lanto, help me develop the discernment to evaluate the energy flow behind spiritual, political, scientific or religious teachings, and behind music and newscasts. Help me detect when the energy waves go up, when they go down or when they move up and down with no decisive direction.

> Beloved Apollo, exposing all lies,
> I hereby surrender all ego-based ties,
> I know my perception is truly the key,
> to transcending the serpentine duality.

> **Beloved Apollo, we heed now your call,**
> **drawing us into Wisdom's Great Hall,**
> **exposing all lies causing the fall,**
> **you help us reclaim the oneness of all.**

4. Master Lanto, help me discern the statements with words that produce an upwards energy flow. Help me see that any statement expressed with words in the material universe can only produce an energy impulse that goes so far.

> Beloved Apollo, your wisdom so clear,
> in oneness with you, no serpent I fear,
> the beam in my eye I'm willing to see,
> I'm free from the serpent's own duality.

> **Beloved Apollo, my eyes now I raise,**
> **I see that the Earth is in a new phase,**
> **I willingly stand in your piercing gaze,**
> **empowered, I exit duality's maze.**

5. Master Lanto, help me see that any statement expressed in words is given for a certain level of consciousness. Any statement is given for one of the 144 possible levels of consciousness found on earth. Any teaching in the world has a limited range.

Cyclopea so dear, the truth you reveal,
the truth that duality's ailments will heal,
your Emerald Light is like a great balm,
my emotional body is perfectly calm.

Cyclopea so dear, in Emerald Sphere,
to vision so clear I always adhere,
in raising perception I shall persevere,
as deep in my heart your truth I revere.

6. Master Lanto, help me discern when a particular outer teaching has taken me as far as it can take me. Help me feel when a teaching begins to be like a wave in the ocean that moves around in a circle.

Cyclopea so dear, with you I unwind,
all negative spirals clouding my mind,
I know pure awareness is truly my core,
the key to becoming the wide-open door.

Cyclopea so dear, clear my inner sight,
empowered, I pierce the soul's fearful night,
through veils of duality I now take flight,
bathed in your penetrating Emerald Light.

7. Master Lanto, help me truly grasp this mechanism with the outer, conscious mind so I can avoid getting into the blind alley of thinking I have to remain loyal to an outer teaching, guru or organization.

Cyclopea so dear, life can only reflect,
the images that my mind does project,
the key to my healing is clearing the mind,
from the images my ego is hiding behind.

> Cyclopea so dear, I want to aim high,
> to your healing flame I ever draw nigh,
> I now see my life through your single eye,
> beyond all disease I AM ready to fly.

8. Master Lanto, help me let go of a certain teaching, guru or organization without any negative reaction. Help me accept that the teaching was never meant to take me any higher. Help me see whether my ego caused me to interpret the teaching as making an empty promise.

> Cyclopea so dear, your Emerald Flame,
> exposes every subtle, dualistic power game,
> including the game of wanting to say,
> that truth is defined in only one way.
>
> Cyclopea so dear, I am feeling the flow,
> as your Living Truth upon me you bestow,
> I know truth transcends all systems below,
> immersed in your light, I continue to grow.

9. Master Lanto, help me realize that a teaching is only meant to take me a certain level up. When it has done so, it is time to tune in to this. It is *my* responsibility to tune in to this, and then I need to make the decision to move on.

> Accelerate my Awakeness, I AM real,
> Accelerate my Awakeness, all life heal,
> Accelerate my Awakeness, I AM MORE,
> Accelerate my Awakeness, all will soar.

Accelerate my Awakeness! (3X)
Beloved Apollo and Lumina.
Accelerate my Awakeness! (3X)
Beloved Jophiel and Christine.
Accelerate my Awakeness! (3X)
Beloved Master Lanto.
Accelerate my Awakeness! (3X)
Beloved I AM.

2. I attain the vision of the Fifth Ray

1. When the student is ready, the teacher appears. I am willing to let go of an existing teaching and open my mind to the inner direction from my Christ self and my ascended teachers. I am attuning my outer mind, and I know with my outer mind that I have received new direction.

Jophiel Archangel, in wisdom's great light,
all serpentine lies exposed to my sight.
So subtle the lies that creep through the mind,
yet you are the greatest teacher I find.

Jophiel Archangel, exposing all lies,
Jophiel Archangel, cutting all ties.
Jophiel Archangel, clearing the skies,
Jophiel Archangel, my mind truly flies.

2. Master Lanto, help me develop a sense of how energy flows in my own energy field. Help me sense where I have certain hooks in my consciousness that tie me to a particular teaching on earth.

Jophiel Archangel, your wisdom I hail,
your sword cutting through duality's veil.
As you show the way, I know what is real,
from serpentine doubt, I instantly heal.

Jophiel Archangel, exposing all lies,
Jophiel Archangel, cutting all ties.
Jophiel Archangel, clearing the skies,
Jophiel Archangel, my mind truly flies.

3. Master Lanto, help me see why I am being pulled in different directions. Help me see what I haven't let go of, and why I cannot move with the River of Life.

Jophiel Archangel, your reality,
the best antidote to duality.
No lie can remain in your Presence so clear,
with you on my side, no serpent I fear.

Jophiel Archangel, exposing all lies,
Jophiel Archangel, cutting all ties.
Jophiel Archangel, clearing the skies,
Jophiel Archangel, my mind truly flies.

4. Master Lanto, I want to be free from all ties to the past or to any outer thing on earth. I am willing to see these ties with my conscious mind and make the conscious decision to cut the tie.

Jophiel Archangel, God's mind is in me,
and through your clear light, its wisdom I see.
Divisions all vanish, as I see the One,
and truly, the wholeness of mind I have won.

> Jophiel Archangel, exposing all lies,
> Jophiel Archangel, cutting all ties.
> Jophiel Archangel, clearing the skies,
> Jophiel Archangel, my mind truly flies.

5. Master Lanto, help me see the ties that I have and cut them at the level of the identity, mental, and emotional bodies. I accept that it is my responsibility to cut them at the level of the conscious mind. I am willing to develop the conscious awareness, to make a conscious effort and to make a conscious decision.

> Raphael Archangel, your light so intense,
> raise me beyond all human pretense.
> Mother Mary and you have a vision so bold,
> to see that our highest potential unfold.

> **Raphael Archangel, for vision I pray,**
> **Raphael Archangel, show me the way,**
> **Raphael Archangel, your emerald ray,**
> **Raphael Archangel, my life a new day.**

6. As I cut these ties consciously, I feel a new sense of freedom, a new sense of being healed of old wounds and conflicts. I realize my ego and the false teachers will try to make me feel like I have to close my conscious mind to the insights I have already gained at higher levels of the mind. Yet I will let go and move on.

> Raphael Archangel, in emerald sphere,
> to immaculate vision I always adhere.
> Mother Mary enfolds me in her sacred heart,
> from Mother's true love, I am never apart.

> Raphael Archangel, for vision I pray,
> Raphael Archangel, show me the way,
> Raphael Archangel, your emerald ray,
> Raphael Archangel, my life a new day.

7. I am moving on and I am truly healed. I am healed from the divisions that pull my mind in different directions. I am attaining the higher vision that is the hallmark of the Fifth Ray.

> Raphael Archangel, all ailments you heal,
> each cell in my body in light now you seal.
> Mother Mary's immaculate concept I see,
> perfection of health is real now for me.

> Raphael Archangel, for vision I pray,
> Raphael Archangel, show me the way,
> Raphael Archangel, your emerald ray,
> Raphael Archangel, my life a new day.

8. As I attain this vision, I feel whole. As I feel whole, I am the open door for the healing of others. Master Lanto, show me how to use wisdom to heal my wounds, how to use wisdom to heal others by reasoning with others and by reasoning with myself.

> Raphael Archangel, your light is so real,
> the vision of Christ in me you reveal.
> Mother Mary now helps me to truly transcend,
> in emerald light with you I ascend.

> Raphael Archangel, for vision I pray,
> Raphael Archangel, show me the way,
> Raphael Archangel, your emerald ray,
> Raphael Archangel, my life a new day.

9. Master Lanto, help me see that the true purpose of the dictations given by the ascended masters is to give me tools for reasoning with myself at the level of the conscious mind.

> With angels I soar,
> as I reach for MORE.
> The angels so real,
> their love all will heal.
> The angels bring peace,
> all conflicts will cease.
> With angels of light,
> we soar to new height.
>
> **The rustling sound of angel wings,**
> **what joy as even matter sings,**
> **what joy as every atom rings,**
> **in harmony with angel wings.**

3. I accept that I am healed

1. When I study a dictation, I receive spiritual light, and this light begins to create a transformation in my energy field. I also receive outer knowledge in the form of words. The words either stir something in me or they generate a reaction of resistance to the statement.

> Master Lanto, golden wise,
> expose in me the ego's lies.
> Master Lanto, will to be,
> I will to win my mastery.

> O Holy Spirit, flow through me,
> I am the open door for thee.
> O mighty rushing stream of Light,
> transcendence is my sacred right.

2. Master Lanto, when I feel this resistance, I will see it as an opportunity to use the teaching to start reasoning with myself. When I feel a resistance or an unresolved question concerning a teaching, it is *my* responsibility to explore what the resistance means.

> Master Lanto, balance all,
> for wisdom's balance I do call.
> Master Lanto, help me see,
> that balance is the Golden key.

> O Holy Spirit, flow through me,
> I am the open door for thee.
> O mighty rushing stream of Light,
> transcendence is my sacred right.

3. Master Lanto, help me tune in to the spirit behind the words so I can use it as a frame of reference for exposing the illusions of my ego and the false teachers, the illusions that seek to make me reject a higher understanding.

> Master Lanto, from Above,
> I call forth discerning love.
> Master Lanto, love's not blind,
> through love, God vision I will find.

> O Holy Spirit, flow through me,
> I am the open door for thee.
> O mighty rushing stream of Light,
> transcendence is my sacred right.

4. Master Lanto, help me explore the questions and go deeper and deeper. Help me reason with myself in order to clarify which aspect of my ego, which of the spirits in my consciousness, opposes the teaching.

> Master Lanto, pure I am,
> intentions pure as Christic lamb.
> Master Lanto, I will transcend,
> acceleration now my truest friend.

> O Holy Spirit, flow through me,
> I am the open door for thee.
> O mighty rushing stream of Light,
> transcendence is my sacred right.

5. Master Lanto, help me expose the spirit. Help me expose the belief that created the spirit, the particular dualistic illusion that created the spirit. Help me experience the illusion, and in experiencing it, spontaneously letting it go.

> Master Lanto, I am whole,
> no more division in my soul.
> Master Lanto, healing flame,
> all balance in your sacred name.

> O Holy Spirit, flow through me,
> I am the open door for thee.
> O mighty rushing stream of Light,
> transcendence is my sacred right.

6. Master Lanto, I accept my responsibility as a student of the ascended masters. I know that reading a book and practicing invocations will not work against my free will. I will consciously and deliberately look at the beam, the spirit, in my own eye.

> Master Lanto, serve all life,
> as I transcend all inner strife.
> Master Lanto, peace you give,
> to all who want to truly live.

> **O Holy Spirit, flow through me,**
> **I am the open door for thee.**
> **O mighty rushing stream of Light,**
> **transcendence is my sacred right.**

7. Master Lanto, I will keep looking at the illusions from different angles, probing them with different questions, until I see the very core belief behind the illusion. When I see it in the light of Christ truth, I see that it is unreal, that it is an illusion. At that moment, I have no trouble letting it go.

> Master Lanto, free to be,
> in balanced creativity.
> Master Lanto, we employ,
> your balance as the key to joy.

> **O Holy Spirit, flow through me,**
> **I am the open door for thee.**
> **O mighty rushing stream of Light,**
> **transcendence is my sacred right.**

8. Master Lanto, help me realize and accept that in order to be healed I must let go of the state of being unhealed. I am letting go of the sense that I am not healed. I am entering the state of mind where I am healed, where I am whole.

> Master Lanto, balance all,
> the seven rays upon my call.
> Master Lanto, I take flight,
> my threefold flame a blazing light.

> **O Holy Spirit, flow through me,**
> **I am the open door for thee.**
> **O mighty rushing stream of Light,**
> **transcendence is my sacred right.**

9. Master Lanto, help me let go of the disease or the illusion by seeing it through the Christ mind. I will gain the Christ vision by systematically and consciously challenging the illusions, going towards deeper levels until I find the belief that is preventing me from flowing with the River of Life.

> Lanto dear, your Presence here,
> filling up my inner sphere.
> Life is now a sacred flow,
> God Wisdom I on all bestow.

> **O Holy Spirit, flow through me,**
> **I am the open door for thee.**
> **O mighty rushing stream of Light,**
> **transcendence is my sacred right.**

4. I adopt the mindset of ongoing victory

1. Wholeness comes from giving up the sense of being unwhole. I give up the dream of finding some ultimate truth or ultimate formula or gaining some ultimate ability. Nothing in the material world is ultimate. Nothing is finite. Nothing is the end. Everything is the River of Life that constantly flows on.

> Hilarion, on emerald shore,
> I'm free from all that's gone before.
> Hilarion, I let all go,
> that keeps me out of sacred flow.
>
> **O Holy Spirit, flow through me,**
> **I am the open door for thee.**
> **O mighty rushing stream of Light,**
> **transcendence is my sacred right.**

2. Master Lanto, help me truly integrate this truth and make it easier for myself to walk the path of initiation under the seven rays. Help me feel that I am going from one victory to another every time I pass an initiation.

> Hilarion, the secret key,
> is wisdom's own reality.
> Hilarion, all life is healed,
> the ego's face no more concealed.
>
> **O Holy Spirit, flow through me,**
> **I am the open door for thee.**
> **O mighty rushing stream of Light,**
> **transcendence is my sacred right.**

3. Master Lanto, help me accept that you do not judge me the way I judge myself. I see that it is not your role to take me to the ultimate level of initiation. It is your role to take me through the seven levels represented by the Second Ray initiations and then help me move to the Third Ray.

> Hilarion, your love for life,
> helps me surrender inner strife.
> Hilarion, your loving words,
> thrill my heart like song of birds.

> **O Holy Spirit, flow through me,**
> **I am the open door for thee.**
> **O mighty rushing stream of Light,**
> **transcendence is my sacred right.**

4. Master Lanto, I accept that you do *not* look at me as an inadequate student. You look at me in a positive light. You look at me as a student who has attained the victory of passing through the seven initiations under Master MORE and the First Ray.

> Hilarion, invoke the light,
> your sacred formulas recite.
> Hilarion, your secret tone,
> philosopher's most sacred stone.

> **O Holy Spirit, flow through me,**
> **I am the open door for thee.**
> **O mighty rushing stream of Light,**
> **transcendence is my sacred right.**

5. Master Lanto, I see that you look at me as having won an important victory before I even enter your retreat. When I pass the first level of initiation, I win another important victory and so on. When I get to the final initiation in your retreat, I win the highest victory at your level of initiation, and you are gratified that you can send me on to the next level up.

> Hilarion, with love you greet,
> me in your temple over Crete.
> Hilarion, your emerald light,
> my third eye sees with Christic sight.
>
> **O Holy Spirit, flow through me,**
> **I am the open door for thee.**
> **O mighty rushing stream of Light,**
> **transcendence is my sacred right.**

6. Master Lanto, I see that there is no defeat, there is no inadequacy. When I arrive at your retreat, I have passed the initiations of the First Ray, and that is indeed a victory.

> Hilarion, you give me fruit,
> of truth that is so absolute.
> Hilarion, all stress decrease,
> as my ambitions I release.
>
> **O Holy Spirit, flow through me,**
> **I am the open door for thee.**
> **O mighty rushing stream of Light,**
> **transcendence is my sacred right.**

7. Master Lanto, help me transcend any feeling of being inadequate. I accept that it is a victory that I have passed the difficult and rigorous initiations under the First Ray. It is a victory that I am passing the initiations under the Second Ray.

> Hilarion, my chakras clear,
> as I let go of subtlest fear.
> Hilarion, I am sincere,
> as freedom's truth I do revere.

> **O Holy Spirit, flow through me,**
> **I am the open door for thee.**
> **O mighty rushing stream of Light,**
> **transcendence is my sacred right.**

8. I am willing to experience the Spirit of Truth beyond the outer statement of truth. I am making swift progress and I am passing the fifth level of initiation on the Second Ray.

> Hilarion, you balance all,
> the seven rays upon my call.
> Hilarion, you keep me true,
> as I remain all one with you.

> **O Holy Spirit, flow through me,**
> **I am the open door for thee.**
> **O mighty rushing stream of Light,**
> **transcendence is my sacred right.**

9. I am willing to reason with myself and probe why my ego has this quest for ultimate truth. Master Lanto, help me see the particular belief that makes me vulnerable to this impossible quest. Help me reach the point of clarity where I make the spontaneous decision to let it go.

Hilarion, your Presence here,
filling up my inner sphere.
Life is now a sacred flow,
God Vision I on all bestow.

**O Holy Spirit, flow through me,
I am the open door for thee.
O mighty rushing stream of Light,
transcendence is my sacred right.**

Sealing:

In the name of the Divine Mother, I fully accept that the power of these calls is used to set free the Ma-ter light, so it can outpicture the perfect vision of Christ for my own life, for all people and for the planet. In the name I AM THAT I AM, it is done! Amen.

14 | WISDOM AND PEACE

I AM the Ascended Master Lanto. I come to give you a discourse on the initiations you face at the sixth level of instruction under the Second Ray of God Wisdom. The sixth level corresponds to the Sixth Ray, which has often been called the ray of peace or the ray of service. How can you give true service unless you do so from a state of mind of being at peace? How can you be at peace unless you have attained the wisdom of knowing what is real and what is unreal, what is important and what is not important?

I have talked in previous discourses about the belief, so common on earth, that there must be some superior or ultimate wisdom, some absolute truth. When you look at the concept of wisdom from the dualistic mind, the mind that is based on separation from oneness, then you can look at wisdom in only one way. You look at wisdom as that which divides, for you think that true wisdom is set apart from false wisdom, superior wisdom is set apart from inferior wisdom, absolute wisdom is set apart from relative wisdom. The reality is, however, that everything that is expressed in words is relative wisdom. What does this mean?

The sixth initiation under the Second Ray

What we attempt to show students at the sixth level of my retreat is that it is not wisdom in a worded form, in any worded form, that will get you to the ascended state. I have talked before about how we can make visible on a screen what happens at the energy level. What we do at the sixth level of initiation is that we ask the students to go into the library and pick what they consider to be either the highest wisdom or, at least, a true and valid form of wisdom. When they come back with a book or a scripture, we then show them what happens at an energy level if they use that worded expression of wisdom.

We can show them that their path is like a spiral staircase. We can show them where they are right now. We can then show them the path of light that leads them higher towards the 144th level. We can then show them how the expression of wisdom that they have picked can take them up the staircase but only to a certain level. We can show them how, when they come to that level, their progress will stop. We can show them that, from that point on, the energies that are flowing through their beings cannot be translated into further progress on the path.

The simple reason is that they have now reached the highest level for which that particular teaching was given. You cannot go higher by clinging to the outer teaching and insisting that the light that flows from your I AM Presence should conform to and validate the outer teaching. Your I AM Presence is forever committed to your growth, leading all the way to your ascension and beyond. When you have reached the maximum level of growth that you can reach with a particular teaching, your I AM Presence will give you both light and ideas that go beyond the teaching.

This does not mean that you have to necessarily throw away the teaching, but you have to be willing to let your I AM Presence take you beyond the teaching. This may necessitate that you find a teaching that is given for a higher level of consciousness. It may necessitate that you have no teaching or that you have no teaching for a while. It may even be possible that you can keep a certain teaching and continue to use it as a foundation, but your I AM Presence takes you beyond it so that you develop a deeper understanding than what is expressed in the words of that teaching.

Your I AM Presence can only take you higher when you are willing to question the teaching. If you are not willing to do so, if you are not willing to look beyond, then the I AM Presence will continue to send you light, but the light will now become a factor that will disturb your inner sense of peace or equilibrium. It will disturb the sense that you have developed, namely that you are saved because you are following the highest teaching. There will be an inner pressure that will continue to build, and you will either transcend the outer teaching or at least your approach to it, or you will then do what you see so many religious people having done on earth. You will turn the outer teaching into a weapon to use against others in putting them down and raising yourself up.

Transcend words, don't cling to them

You will see many people who have gone into the dualistic game of seeking to establish their teaching, religion, political philosophy or scientific philosophy as the superior one. They have gone into the state of battling with others. They are convinced that, because they have the superior truth, they must destroy false truths, they must make other people conform. This goal of changing something outside yourself is nothing but camouflage. You will not make your ascension even by getting all people on earth to follow a particular belief system.

The reason for this is simple. You will reach the ascended state *only* by going beyond any and all worded expressions on earth. It does not matter if you have a teaching that is the word of God or is expressed as a dictation by the ascended masters through a sponsored messenger. As I have said before, once the teaching is expressed in words, it is no longer the Living Spirit of Wisdom. You will not ascend by clinging to a worded expression. You will ascend by transcending words and becoming one with the spirit. First, you become one with the spirits behind each of the seven rays. Then you become one with your I AM Presence, your personal spirit.

We can show students on a screen what happens to the energies as they become attached to an outer teaching. Take note of the subtle difference. There is a stage where following an outer teaching helps you grow. It helps you rise up the spiral staircase. There also comes a point where the outer teaching cannot take you further, and it does not matter which outer teaching it is. *Do you understand what I am saying?* Do you grasp this with your outer awareness, with your conscious mind? I can assure you that many students find this difficult to grasp, even when they are at our retreats, and are not quite as colored by their outer minds. It is important that you grasp this with the outer mind.

There is no teaching given in words that corresponds to the 144th level of consciousness. There is no teaching given in words that corresponds to the 143rd or the 142nd. There comes a point, and I will not tell you what that point is, where you have reached a level of consciousness from where no worded teaching can take you higher. You must, at that point, go beyond words and make direct inner contact with the spirit behind the worded teaching. If you do not make this contact, you cannot go higher. This is to make sure that you cannot go beyond a certain level while retaining elements of the consciousness of separation, the consciousness of duality, the desire to put others down in order to raise yourself up.

When a student grasps this reality, a big burden is lifted from the student's shoulders. Suddenly, he or she feels a greater sense of peace, for now the student knows that it does not have to go out and battle other belief systems. The student becomes aware that there are many belief systems on earth that can take people to higher levels of consciousness. It truly does not matter which one of these valid systems a person is following, as long as the person is growing. You cannot with your outer mind – at least not until you have reached a very high level of consciousness – judge whether other people are growing or whether they should be following this or that outer teaching.

You cannot force oneness

Take an honest look at the spiritual movements you have found, that you have been involved with. Take a look and see how many of them have this sense of exclusivity that they have the highest teaching or the highest guru, and that it is necessary to convert the world to their viewpoint. Take a look and see how tense people are when they go into this mindset. On the one hand, it offers the ego a great sense of superiority because you belong to this ultimate teaching, but on the other hand, it puts you in constant conflict with those who are not in the teaching.

What happens when you see yourself as being in conflict with others? Well, you cannot come into oneness with them, can you? What is the goal of the spiritual path? It is that you reach up for the Alpha aspect of oneness with your I AM Presence, oneness with the spirit, and then, you reach out horizontally, seeking to establish oneness with other people.

How can you be one with others if you are seeking to force them to enter a particular teaching? This cannot be done. Oneness cannot be forced. It is the natural state that occurs when you rise above the consciousness of force and make a conscious decision to enter oneness. You cannot make that decision as long as you are seeking to force others or even force yourself. We aim to show students that when you think there is a superior form of wisdom, then you are not only seeking to force others, you are actually forcing yourself. You have to live up to the outer teaching. You have to follow the outer teaching, often in a rather literal and linear way. This is where we come to another dividing line. Students will not move to the seventh level of our retreat until they pass this initiation. We have talked about a spiritual path.

We have talked about you walking a path from a certain level of consciousness towards higher and higher levels, until you reach the ultimate level and can ascend. We have compared the spiritual path to a spiral staircase, and you know very well that you can walk up a spiral staircase by taking one step at a time. This is a very linear process. You are on one step. You lift your foot and put it on the next step. You lift your second foot and pull it up, and now you are at a higher step. You do the same again, and you are at the next step up. You can continue to do this one step at a time until you reach the top of the spiral staircase. The path of initiation has a series of linear steps, but you do not pass the initiation represented by each step by being in the linear state of consciousness. You pass the initiation only by going beyond the linear form of thinking, the linear mind.

The quantum leap in consciousness

You have heard of the concept of a quantum leap. What is a quantum leap? It is a shift from one state to the next. You may say that a larva turns itself into a cocoon, and after some time turns itself into a butterfly. If you look at a larva, you cannot say that there is a linear progression from the larva stage to the cocoon stage, nor is there a linear progression from the cocoon to the butterfly. It is not a logical, a linear and necessary, evolution of the cocoon to become a butterfly. It is a quantum leap from the cocoon to the butterfly. You may look at a bird's nest and see an egg. You can do what science has done and you can

14 | Wisdom and Peace

show how inside the egg grows the chick. The chick becomes bigger and more developed until one day it breaks out of the shell and now starts walking like a chick, instead of the embryo inside the egg. From the inside, this is not a linear progression. The chick must make a quantum leap in consciousness in order to break the shell and enter the next stage.

You may look at a bird's nest and see how the chick grows bigger and bigger. Its feathers grow out. Its wings become longer and longer. You may look at the chick sitting on the nest flapping its wings, but a chick sitting on the nest flapping its wings is not a flying bird. What does the bird need to do to actually fly? It needs to make a quantum leap in consciousness, and from the moment it leaves the nest, it is no longer a chick, it is the full-fledged bird.

We are seeking to help you walk the path of initiation by portraying this path as a linear progression from lower to higher levels of consciousness. We are seeking to take a student who comes to our retreat by the hand, and put it through various initiations, give it various exercises and various statements of wisdom, in order to take that student to the point where it is ready to take the initiation and rise to the next level of consciousness.

Even though we are attempting to take the student gradually, a student cannot actually move from one level to the next as a linear process. Every time a student is ready at one level, and then has the potential to go to the next level, the student must make a quantum leap of consciousness. We have said before that you must actually let the sense of self you have at a given step die. For an interval beyond time, you have no fixed sense of self, and then, you are reborn into a higher sense of self. Most people do not realize this in their waking consciousness. You have actually gone through it many times in your life. Many of the important turning points in your life have been events where you took a quantum leap of consciousness. Most people do not realize this with the conscious mind. They make the shift without actually realizing that the old sense of self has died, and they have been reborn into a new sense of self. This is because the mind creates a sense of continuity.

We may say that this sense of continuity is the basic, core aspect of the ego. We may say that, when you reach the 144th level, the initiation you face is that you must let go of all sense of continuity in order to actually ascend. The ascension is not a linear progression from the unascended state of consciousness. It is a quantum leap beyond it. This is the ultimate quantum leap that you can take in the material universe, and that is why we are attempting to take you through 144 steps of smaller quantum leaps in order to prepare you for the ultimate leap. At the sixth level, you need to make a quantum leap, for you realize that wisdom can either help you grow or it can become the ultimate trap that hinders your growth.

Overcome value judgments to attain peace

What did the Buddha answer when the people seeing him sitting in Nirvana asked: "What are you?" They meant: "Are you a man or are you a god?" What did the Buddha answer? He did not say he was a man; he did not say he was not a man. He did not say he was a god; he did not say he was not a god. He said: "I am awake." Take note of what he also did not say. He did not say: "I am a Buddhist," nor did he say: "I am a Buddha." What did he attempt to communicate by saying "I am awake"? He attempted to communicate that he had gone beyond the state of consciousness where you need to label everything. This is the key to peace.

When you look at life through the consciousness of duality and separation, you must label everything that you observe, everything that happens. This is natural. There is nothing inherently wrong in it, for this is how you grow from one level of consciousness to the next. You are coming to the realization that you have so far had a certain belief. You are realizing that there is a stage above that belief, and you are deciding to let go of the old and embrace the higher.

What the ego and the false teachers attempt to do is to make you add a value judgment to this labeling process. It says: "This is good; this is evil. This is ultimate; this is inferior" If you say: "This is white and this is black," you are labeling. You are discriminating between two different forms, but saying something is white and black is not saying that it is good or bad. Ice is white; coal is black. Does it make any sense to say that coal is evil and ice is good? The white ice may indeed kill you whereas the black coal may be burned and warm you and save your life.

What we aim to show students is that it is perfectly acceptable at this level to take a statement of wisdom, an outer teaching, and accept that this is the vehicle that you have chosen to use for your growth. It is, however, not acceptable at this level to maintain the value judgment that this teaching is better than all others, and you must continue to cling to it for the rest of your path.

Do you, perhaps, understand with the outer mind a very profound realization? We have seen many students who have found a teaching given by us over this last century or more where we have openly made our existence known as ascended masters. We have seen them find a specific teaching given through a specific messenger or organization, and we have seen them reason that now they must have found the ultimate teaching. The teachings we have given have been valid. They have been at varying degrees of purity, and they have been aimed at varying levels of consciousness, but they have been valid. They are still valid.

Many students have reasoned that this is not just one valid teaching. It is the ultimate teaching, and therefore all people must be converted to that teaching. They think that we, who are the ascended masters, actually have as our goal to convert everyone on earth to consciously following the teachings of the ascended masters. This is not the case at all.

There are also those students who believe that only people who, with their conscious minds, accept the existence of ascended masters and an outer teaching can come to our retreats at night. Right now, here in the Royal Teton Retreat, I have students who come from all parts of the world, all cultures, all religions, many who have no outer religion at all. I have some who in their outer minds are agnostics, atheists or materialists.

We of the ascended masters do not base our work on the outer beliefs and behavior of the students. We look at the inner conditions of the lifestream, and we simply evaluate: Is a certain lifestream ready for the initiations that I, Lanto, offer at the first level of the Royal Teton Retreat? If so, that student is welcome in its finer bodies to come to the retreat. When they do come here, it is not my goal that they should always come to an outer recognition of the existence of ascended masters or a particular outer teaching or organization and then follow that teaching or join the organization.

We have many students who are following the path in our retreats, but it is perfectly acceptable at this level that they belong to a particular outer culture, religion or belief system—or no religion or belief system. As long as the student is following the path of initiation, it can very well express its growth, its higher level of consciousness, through many different outer cultures or belief systems.

To achieve peace, do not try to convert others

This is a reality that can be very difficult for ascended master students to accept, especially with their conscious minds. When you do accept it, you will find that a great burden is lifted from you. You will realize that you have actually been trapped by this idea of having to convert others because it puts a distance between you and others and it creates a tension. You are the one who feels that tension more than other people feel it, for you, of course, experience it from inside your own mind and that, my beloved, is where the tension is found. The other people may also have a tension, but *their* tension is located in *their* minds. *Your* growth on the spiritual path does not depend on whether *they* overcome their tension or not. It does, however, depend on whether *you* overcome *your own* inner tension.

What you need to do at this level, the sixth level on the Second Ray, is that you need to become aware of this tension, and then, you need to make a conscious effort to let go of it. When you let go of this tension, it becomes so much easier for you to be who you are and to talk about your spiritual beliefs and knowledge. You are not doing it for the purpose of converting others or proving their view wrong. You are sharing what you believe, the insights that you have come to and why and how you came to those insights. You are sharing for the purpose of sharing, not for the purpose of converting or forcing. You are not seeking to put other people's beliefs down, label them or put a value judgment upon them. You are sharing your own, and you can do this with the love, joy and enthusiasm that actually is the best way to convert others.

How will you be at peace, if you think you have to convert others to your superior form of wisdom? How will you be at peace if you think you can attain this goal only by taking the fear-based approach or tearing down their present beliefs and trying to make them believe that they are false and will take them to hell? How can you come into oneness with others if you think they will go to hell unless they accept your view, your outer expression of wisdom? You can come into oneness with others only when you have come into oneness with the Spirit of Wisdom. You seek to help others come into oneness with the Spirit of Wisdom rather than seeking to force them to come into compliance with an outer expression of wisdom.

It is very true that when the Buddha made the statement: "I am awake," he was quite aware that many people on earth would not see this as a significant statement. They would not realize that they are not awake. They would not want to awaken. They would want to remain in their unawakened state because this was the experience they wanted to have. The Buddha did not have as the goal to convert all people on earth to an outer wisdom or religion. He knew that only *some* would understand.

You should know the same. You do not have to convert or convince everyone. You do not have to come into oneness with everyone, for many are still so attached to the consciousness of separation that they want no part of oneness with you or anyone else. You only have to share your Presence, your being, your wisdom, your insights, and then seek to come into oneness with those who *do* understand, those who *do* appreciate because they have come to some of the same realizations.

Be at peace with your current level of consciousness

Be not concerned about converting others to an outer ascended master teaching or organization. Make a conscious effort to let go of this belief and give yourself permission to be who you are and to be at peace in knowing that being who you are is enough. Sharing who you are at this level of the path is all you are required to do at this level of the path. You are, of course, meant to continue to rise to higher and higher levels of the path, but you cannot, when you come to the sixth level of initiation under the Second Ray, rise to the next level until you are at peace with being where you are at and sharing your insights at this level of consciousness, letting that be enough.

You will think I am contradicting myself, at least your outer mind will think so. You will think I am telling you to continue to rise in consciousness, and you will think this means that you cannot be satisfied that where you are at is enough. You are, of course, right. You cannot rise higher until you desire something more than what you have, more than the level of consciousness you are at. What did I say about the quantum leap?

The seventh level of initiation is not a linear progression from the sixth level; it is a quantum leap above it. You will not be able to make that quantum leap until you have made peace with being at the sixth level, which is the initiation of peace. You will not be able to rise to the seventh level until you are at peace with the wisdom you have and not seeking to use it with force to generate conflict.

You will rise to the seventh level when you give up the desire to force a particular expression of wisdom upon others, and thereby set yourself free to be at peace in the wisdom you have. When you are at peace in the wisdom you have, you can also be at peace in giving up that wisdom. You can look me, Lanto, straight in the eye and say: "Master, I want more. I want the next level of initiation, but I am at peace in being where I am, and I leave it to you to decide when I am ready."

When you decide that you will leave the decision to me instead of judging yourself with the outer mind, then you are ready to take the next step. Until you are willing to let me be the master and you be the student, you will not be ready. You might be sitting at the edge of the nest flapping your wings with great force, but you will not have liftoff. You will not have the inner peace of knowing that when you push off from the nest, your wings will, indeed, carry you through the air.

Lanto I AM, and I AM at peace in the wisdom that I AM.

15 | I INVOKE BUDDHIC WISDOM

In the name I AM THAT I AM, Jesus Christ, I call to my I AM Presence to flow through the I Will Be Presence that I AM and give this invocation with full power. I call to beloved Elohim Apollo and Lumina and Peace and Aloha, Archangel Jophiel and Christine and Uriel and Aurora, Master Lanto and Nada to help me accept that where I am at on the path is good enough while still striving to move on. Help me see and surrender all patterns that block my oneness with Master Lanto and my oneness with my I AM Presence, including …

[Make personal calls]

1. I will ascend by going beyond words

1. Master Lanto, help me give true service from a state of mind of being at peace. Help me be at peace by attaining the wisdom of knowing what is real and what is unreal, what is important and what is not important.

Beloved Apollo, with your second ray,
you open my eyes to see a new day,
I see through duality's lies and deceit,
transcending the mindset producing defeat.

**Beloved Apollo, thou Elohim Gold,
your radiant light my eyes now behold,
as pages of wisdom you gently unfold,
I feel I am free from all that is old.**

2. Master Lanto, help me transcend the dualistic mindset of looking at wisdom as that which divides, of thinking that true wisdom is set apart from false wisdom. Help me experience that everything that is expressed in words is relative wisdom.

Beloved Apollo, in your flame I know,
that your living wisdom is always a flow,
in your light I see my own highest will,
immersed in the stream that never stands still.

**Beloved Apollo, your light makes it clear,
why we have taken embodiment here,
working to raise our own cosmic sphere,
together we form the tip of the spear.**

3. Master Lanto, help me transcend the ego-based tendency to demand that the light from my I AM Presence should conform to and validate an outer teaching. My I AM Presence is forever committed to my growth, leading all the way to my ascension and beyond.

> Beloved Apollo, exposing all lies,
> I hereby surrender all ego-based ties,
> I know my perception is truly the key,
> to transcending the serpentine duality.
>
> **Beloved Apollo, we heed now your call,**
> **drawing us into Wisdom's Great Hall,**
> **exposing all lies causing the fall,**
> **you help us reclaim the oneness of all.**

4. Master Lanto, help me accept that when I have reached the maximum level of growth that I can reach with a particular teaching, my I AM Presence will give me both light and ideas that go beyond the teaching.

> Beloved Apollo, your wisdom so clear,
> in oneness with you, no serpent I fear,
> the beam in my eye I'm willing to see,
> I'm free from the serpent's own duality.
>
> **Beloved Apollo, my eyes now I raise,**
> **I see that the Earth is in a new phase,**
> **I willingly stand in your piercing gaze,**
> **empowered, I exit duality's maze.**

5. I am willing to let my I AM Presence take me higher. I am willing to question my outer teaching. I realize that if I do not, my I AM Presence will continue to send me light that will disturb my sense of equilibrium.

> O Elohim Peace, in Unity's Flame,
> there is no more room for duality's game,
> we know that all form is from the same source,
> empowering us to plot a new course.

> O Elohim Peace, the bell now you ring,
> causing all atoms to vibrate and sing,
> I now see that there is no separate thing,
> to my ego-based self I no longer cling.

6. Master Lanto, help me see that I will not make my ascension by getting all people on earth to follow a particular belief system. I will reach the ascended state *only* by going beyond any and all worded expressions on earth.

> O Elohim Peace, you help me to know,
> that Jesus has come your Flame to bestow,
> upon all who are ready to give up the strife,
> by following Christ into infinite life.

> O Elohim Peace, through your eyes I see,
> that only in oneness will I ever be free,
> I give up the sense of a separate me,
> I AM crossing Samsara's turbulent sea.

7. Master Lanto, help me see that I will ascend by transcending words and becoming one with the spirit. First, I become one with the spirits behind each of the seven rays. Then I become one with my I AM Presence, my personal spirit.

> O Elohim Peace, you show me the way,
> for clearing my mind from duality's fray,
> you pierce the illusions of both time and space,
> separation consumed by your Infinite Grace.

> O Elohim Peace, what beauty your name,
> consuming within me duality's shame,
> It was through the vibration of your Golden Flame,
> that Christ the illusion of death overcame.

8. Master Lanto, help me grasp with my outer awareness, with my conscious mind, the need to let my I AM Presence take me higher. Help me attain the greater sense of peace that comes from knowing that I do not have to go out and battle other belief systems.

> O Elohim Peace, you bring now to Earth,
> the unstoppable flame of Cosmic Rebirth,
> I give up the sense that something is mine,
> allowing your Light through my being to shine.

> **O Elohim Peace, through your tranquility,**
> **we are free from the chaos of duality,**
> **in oneness with God a new identity,**
> **we are raising the Earth into Infinity.**

9. Master Lanto, help me see that my outer mind cannot judge whether other people are growing or whether they should be following this or that outer teaching. When I see myself as being in conflict with others, I cannot come into oneness with them. The goal of the spiritual path is oneness with my I AM Presence and oneness with other people.

> Accelerate my Awakeness, I AM real,
> Accelerate my Awakeness, all life heal,
> Accelerate my Awakeness, I AM MORE,
> Accelerate my Awakeness, all will soar.

Accelerate my Awakeness! (3X)
Beloved Apollo and Lumina.
Accelerate my Awakeness! (3X)
Beloved Jophiel and Christine.
Accelerate my Awakeness! (3X)
Beloved Master Lanto.
Accelerate my Awakeness! (3X)
Beloved I AM.

2. I will make the quantum leap

1. Oneness cannot be forced. It is the natural state that occurs when I rise above the consciousness of force and make a conscious decision to enter oneness. I cannot make that decision as long as I am seeking to force others or even force myself.

Jophiel Archangel, in wisdom's great light,
all serpentine lies exposed to my sight.
So subtle the lies that creep through the mind,
yet you are the greatest teacher I find.

Jophiel Archangel, exposing all lies,
Jophiel Archangel, cutting all ties.
Jophiel Archangel, clearing the skies,
Jophiel Archangel, my mind truly flies.

2. Master Lanto, help me see that when I think there is a superior form of wisdom, then I am not only seeking to force others, I am forcing myself. I have to live up to the outer teaching. I have to follow the outer teaching in a literal and linear way.

Jophiel Archangel, your wisdom I hail,
your sword cutting through duality's veil.
As you show the way, I know what is real,
from serpentine doubt, I instantly heal.

**Jophiel Archangel, exposing all lies,
Jophiel Archangel, cutting all ties.
Jophiel Archangel, clearing the skies,
Jophiel Archangel, my mind truly flies.**

3. The path of initiation has a series of linear steps, but I do not pass the initiation represented by each step by being in the linear state of consciousness. I pass the initiation only by going beyond the linear form of thinking, the linear mind.

Jophiel Archangel, your reality,
the best antidote to duality.
No lie can remain in your Presence so clear,
with you on my side, no serpent I fear.

**Jophiel Archangel, exposing all lies,
Jophiel Archangel, cutting all ties.
Jophiel Archangel, clearing the skies,
Jophiel Archangel, my mind truly flies.**

4. Each step on the path requires me to make a quantum leap, a shift from one state to the next. I am willing to let the sense of self I have at my present step die. For an interval beyond time, I will have no fixed sense of self, and then I am reborn into a higher sense of self.

> Jophiel Archangel, God's mind is in me,
> and through your clear light, its wisdom I see.
> Divisions all vanish, as I see the One,
> and truly, the wholeness of mind I have won.
>
> **Jophiel Archangel, exposing all lies,**
> **Jophiel Archangel, cutting all ties.**
> **Jophiel Archangel, clearing the skies,**
> **Jophiel Archangel, my mind truly flies.**

5. Master Lanto, help me see that I have gone through this shift many times in my life. Many of the important turning points in my life have been events where I took a quantum leap of consciousness. I do not normally see this because the mind creates a sense of continuity.

> Uriel Archangel, immense is the power,
> of angels of peace, all war to devour.
> The demons of war, no match for your light,
> consuming them all, with radiance so bright.
>
> **Uriel Archangel, use your great sword,**
> **Uriel Archangel, consume all discord,**
> **Uriel Archangel, we're of one accord,**
> **Uriel Archangel, we walk with the Lord.**

6. Master Lanto, help me see that this sense of continuity is the basic, core aspect of the ego. When I reach the 144th level, the initiation I face is that I must let go of all sense of continuity in order to actually ascend. The ascension is not a linear progression from the unascended state of consciousness. It is a quantum leap beyond it.

Uriel Archangel, intense is the sound,
when millions of angels, their voices compound.
They build a crescendo, piercing the night,
life's glorious oneness revealed to our sight.

Uriel Archangel, use your great sword,
Uriel Archangel, consume all discord,
Uriel Archangel, we're of one accord,
Uriel Archangel, we walk with the Lord.

7. Master Lanto, help me make the quantum leap at the sixth level by realizing that wisdom can either help me grow or it can become the ultimate trap that hinders my growth.

Uriel Archangel, from out the Great Throne,
your millions of trumpets, sound the One Tone.
Consuming all discord with your harmony,
the sound of all sounds will set all life free.

Uriel Archangel, use your great sword,
Uriel Archangel, consume all discord,
Uriel Archangel, we're of one accord,
Uriel Archangel, we walk with the Lord.

8. Master Lanto, help me see that when the Buddha said: "I am awake," he attempted to communicate that he had gone beyond the state of consciousness where you need to label everything. This is the key to peace.

Uriel Archangel, all war is now gone,
for you bring a message, from heart of the One.
The hearts of all men, now singing in peace,
the spirals of love, forever increase.

**Uriel Archangel, use your great sword,
Uriel Archangel, consume all discord,
Uriel Archangel, we're of one accord,
Uriel Archangel, we walk with the Lord.**

9. Master Lanto, help me see that at a certain stage of the path, labeling everything that I observe is natural. Yet the ego and the false teachers attempt to make me add a value judgment of good and evil to this labeling process.

With angels I soar,
as I reach for MORE.
The angels so real,
their love all will heal.
The angels bring peace,
all conflicts will cease.
With angels of light,
we soar to new height.

**The rustling sound of angel wings,
what joy as even matter sings,
what joy as every atom rings,
in harmony with angel wings.**

3. I transcend all desire to convert others

1. Master Lanto, help me see that it is constructive to take an outer teaching and accept that this is the vehicle I have chosen for my growth. It is *not* constructive to maintain the value judgment that this teaching is better than all others.

Master Lanto, golden wise,
expose in me the ego's lies.
Master Lanto, will to be,
I will to win my mastery.

**O Holy Spirit, flow through me,
I am the open door for thee.
O mighty rushing stream of Light,
transcendence is my sacred right.**

2. Master Lanto, help me see that the ascended masters do not base their work on the outer beliefs and behavior of the students. You look at the inner conditions of the lifestream and evaluate: Is a certain lifestream ready for the initiations offered?

Master Lanto, balance all,
for wisdom's balance I do call.
Master Lanto, help me see,
that balance is the Golden key.

**O Holy Spirit, flow through me,
I am the open door for thee.
O mighty rushing stream of Light,
transcendence is my sacred right.**

3. Master Lanto, help me see that as long as a student is following the path of initiation, it can express its higher level of consciousness through many different outer cultures or belief systems.

Master Lanto, from Above,
I call forth discerning love.
Master Lanto, love's not blind,
through love, God vision I will find.

> O Holy Spirit, flow through me,
> I am the open door for thee.
> O mighty rushing stream of Light,
> transcendence is my sacred right.

4. Master Lanto, help me accept this reality with my conscious mind. Help me realize that I have been trapped by the idea of having to convert others. This puts a distance between me and others and it creates a tension.

> Master Lanto, pure I am,
> intentions pure as Christic lamb.
> Master Lanto, I will transcend,
> acceleration now my truest friend.

> **O Holy Spirit, flow through me,**
> **I am the open door for thee.**
> **O mighty rushing stream of Light,**
> **transcendence is my sacred right.**

5. Master Lanto, help me become aware of the tension that exists inside my own mind. My growth on the spiritual path depends on whether *I* overcome *my own* inner tension.

> Master Lanto, I am whole,
> no more division in my soul.
> Master Lanto, healing flame,
> all balance in your sacred name.

> **O Holy Spirit, flow through me,**
> **I am the open door for thee.**
> **O mighty rushing stream of Light,**
> **transcendence is my sacred right.**

6. Master Lanto, help me become aware of this tension and I will make a conscious effort to let go of it. When I let go of this tension, it becomes so much easier for me to be who I am and to talk about my spiritual beliefs and knowledge.

> Master Lanto, serve all life,
> as I transcend all inner strife.
> Master Lanto, peace you give,
> to all who want to truly live.

> **O Holy Spirit, flow through me,**
> **I am the open door for thee.**
> **O mighty rushing stream of Light,**
> **transcendence is my sacred right.**

7. I surrender the desire to convert others or prove their view wrong. I am sharing what I believe, the insights I have come to and why and how I came to those insights. I am sharing with the love and joy and enthusiasm that is the best way to convert others.

> Master Lanto, free to be,
> in balanced creativity.
> Master Lanto, we employ,
> your balance as the key to joy.

> **O Holy Spirit, flow through me,**
> **I am the open door for thee.**
> **O mighty rushing stream of Light,**
> **transcendence is my sacred right.**

8. Master Lanto, help me see that I cannot be at peace if I think I have to convert others to my superior form of wisdom. I cannot be at peace by taking the fear-based approach of tearing down the beliefs of others and trying to make them believe that they are false and will take them to hell.

> Master Lanto, balance all,
> the seven rays upon my call.
> Master Lanto, I take flight,
> my threefold flame a blazing light.

> **O Holy Spirit, flow through me,**
> **I am the open door for thee.**
> **O mighty rushing stream of Light,**
> **transcendence is my sacred right.**

9. I can come into oneness with others only when I have come into oneness with the Spirit of Wisdom. I seek to help others come into oneness with the Spirit of Wisdom rather than seeking to force them to come into compliance with an outer expression of wisdom.

> Lanto dear, your Presence here,
> filling up my inner sphere.
> Life is now a sacred flow,
> God Wisdom I on all bestow.

> **O Holy Spirit, flow through me,**
> **I am the open door for thee.**
> **O mighty rushing stream of Light,**
> **transcendence is my sacred right.**

4. I am the student, Lanto is the master

1. Master Lanto, help me realize that I am not awake. I truly want to awaken, I want to transcend my unawakened state. I want to be one of the people who understands the Buddha.

> Master Nada, beauty's power,
> unfolding like a sacred flower.
> Master Nada, so sublime,
> a will that conquers even time.

> **O Holy Spirit, flow through me,**
> **I am the open door for thee.**
> **O mighty rushing stream of Light,**
> **transcendence is my sacred right.**

2. I am sharing my Presence, my being, my wisdom, my insights. I am seeking to come into oneness with those who *do* understand, those who *do* appreciate because they have come to some of the same realizations.

> Master Nada, you bestow,
> upon me wisdom's rushing flow.
> Master Nada, mind so strong
> rising on your wings of song.

> **O Holy Spirit, flow through me,**
> **I am the open door for thee.**
> **O mighty rushing stream of Light,**
> **transcendence is my sacred right.**

3. I surrender the desire for converting others to an outer ascended master teaching or organization. I am consciously giving myself permission to be who I am and to be at peace in knowing that being who I am is enough. Sharing who I am at this level of the path is all I am required to do at this level of the path.

> Master Nada, precious scent,
> your love is truly heaven-sent.
> Master Nada, kind and soft
> on wings of love we rise aloft.

> **O Holy Spirit, flow through me,**
> **I am the open door for thee.**
> **O mighty rushing stream of Light,**
> **transcendence is my sacred right.**

4. I will continue to rise to higher levels of the path, but when I come to the sixth level of initiation under the Second Ray, I cannot rise to the next level until I am at peace with being where I am at and sharing my insights at this level of consciousness, letting that be enough.

> Master Nada, mother light,
> my heart is rising like a kite.
> Master Nada, from your view,
> all life is pure as morning dew.

> **O Holy Spirit, flow through me,**
> **I am the open door for thee.**
> **O mighty rushing stream of Light,**
> **transcendence is my sacred right.**

5. Master Lanto, help me solve the seeming contradiction of continuing to rise in consciousness while being satisfied that where I am at is enough.

> Master Nada, truth you bring,
> as morning birds in love do sing.
> Master Nada, I now feel,
> your love that all four bodies heal.

> **O Holy Spirit, flow through me,**
> **I am the open door for thee.**
> **O mighty rushing stream of Light,**
> **transcendence is my sacred right.**

6. Master Lanto, help me see that I will not make the quantum leap to the next level until I have made peace with being at the sixth level, which is the initiation of peace. I will not be able to rise to the seventh level until I am at peace with the wisdom I have and not seeking to use it with force to generate conflict.

> Master Nada, serve in peace,
> as all emotions I release.
> Master Nada, life is fun,
> my solar plexus is a sun.

> **O Holy Spirit, flow through me,**
> **I am the open door for thee.**
> **O mighty rushing stream of Light,**
> **transcendence is my sacred right.**

7. I give up the desire to force a particular expression of wisdom upon others. I am setting myself free to be at peace in the wisdom I have. When I am at peace in the wisdom I have, I can also be at peace in giving up that wisdom.

Master Nada, love is free,
with no conditions binding me.
Master Nada, rise above,
all human forms of lesser love.

**O Holy Spirit, flow through me,
I am the open door for thee.
O mighty rushing stream of Light,
transcendence is my sacred right.**

8. Master Lanto, I am looking you straight in the eye and I say: "Master, I want more. I want the next level of initiation, but I am at peace in being where I am, and I leave it to you to decide when I am ready."

Master Nada, balance all,
the seven rays upon my call.
Master Nada, rise and shine,
your radiant beauty most divine.

**O Holy Spirit, flow through me,
I am the open door for thee.
O mighty rushing stream of Light,
transcendence is my sacred right.**

9. Master Lanto, I am willing to let you be the master and I be the student. I have the inner peace of knowing that when I push off from the nest, my wings will, indeed, carry me through the air.

Nada Dear, your Presence here,
filling up my inner sphere.
Life is now a sacred flow,
God Peace on all I do bestow.

**O Holy Spirit, flow through me,
I am the open door for thee.
O mighty rushing stream of Light,
transcendence is my sacred right.**

Sealing:

In the name of the Divine Mother, I fully accept that the power of these calls is used to set free the Ma-ter light, so it can outpicture the perfect vision of Christ for my own life, for all people and for the planet. In the name I AM THAT I AM, it is done! Amen.

16 | WISDOM AND FREEDOM

Lanto I AM, and I AM free
because I know reality.

The seventh level of initiation at the Royal Teton Retreat is, of course, about freedom. How does freedom relate to wisdom? There are those who will say that you can only be free when you have the highest wisdom, the ultimate wisdom. There are those who will say that freedom can only come when you accept the highest wisdom.

The unreality of dualistic belief systems

You may take almost any belief system on earth, and you will see that those who are the linear followers of that system say that those who know the system – those who accept its doctrines, dogmas and wisdom – they are free. All others are enslaved by ignorance, by the devil or whatever the system defines as the adversary. Truly, there *is* an adversary, but the adversary is unreal. The adversary is not what most belief systems on earth make him out to be, namely the opposite of the good, the opposite of God. As we have said many times in various teachings, the duality consciousness creates two opposite polarities that exist only in relation to each other. What most belief systems on earth define as good and what they define as evil both spring from the duality consciousness.

Even if a belief system labels the good as God, it is not the real God, the formless, transcendent God. It is a god that has been given form by the system, that has been defined by the system. Of course, the system was defined by those in separation, meaning the false hierarchy of the false teachers on earth. They have used the duality consciousness to define a system, to define God within the system, and then to elevate this system to the ultimate authority by claiming that it has the ultimate definition of God.

Anytime you think you can define God by words on planet earth, you are demonstrating that you do not have true wisdom. You only have the false, relative, dualistic wisdom where you have created your own system that seeks to define wisdom. Having such a system offers certain advantages, especially to people who are below the 48th level of consciousness. If you want to feel superior to others, if you want to feel that you and your group alone are being saved and all others will be condemned to an eternity in hell, then you need such a system. When you become an ascended master student and have it as your goal to climb from the 48th to the 96th level of consciousness, then you cannot continue to hold on to this approach to wisdom, this approach to wanting to define some ultimate truth. You cannot be free in expressing wisdom if you always have to compare it to something defined with words.

Be the open door for the Spirit of Wisdom

What have I said is the ultimate key to really knowing wisdom? It is to go beyond the worded systems on earth and tune in – inside yourself – to the Spirit of Wisdom. Until you experience that spirit – as the Conscious You can do when it steps outside the perception filter of the outer self – then you do not know wisdom. If you do not know wisdom, why would you then seek to force what can only be a limited vision upon others? Why would you set yourself up as the judge of others?

Of course, you can set yourself up as such a judge, but then you really cannot be a true ascended master student at the same time. You may claim to be an ascended master student who has the superior wisdom in a particular ascended master teaching, but you are not a true student. You are one of the false students. You have simply used one of our outer teachings expressed in words to validate your view of the false path.

We, of course, are not fooled by this. People on earth may be fooled by it. We certainly know that there are many people who claim to be our students and who have fooled themselves, and even fooled certain others, into thinking they have some superior ascended master wisdom. If you are using your wisdom as a weapon against others, you demonstrate that you have only *outer* wisdom. You have not locked in to the spirit, and therefore you are not free. How do you know with the outer mind what the Spirit of Wisdom desires to express through you in a particular situation? If you are always demanding that before any expression of wisdom can come through you, it must be compared to an outer system and it must conform to that outer system, then what room do you give the spirit?

You may say: "But I have an ascended master teaching that was given by a sponsored messenger. It must be a valid teaching." Certainly, it may, indeed, be a valid teaching. It was valid at the time it was given because it was an expression of the Spirit of Wisdom or another spirit at the time. It was given for a certain level of consciousness. It is most likely still valid for people at that level of consciousness and below it, but how do you know what the Spirit of Wisdom decides, desires, to express today, through you or someone else?

How ascended masters work with organizations

We see, all the time, people who claim to be ascended master students and who have adopted a particular ascended master organization or teaching as their primary teaching. They believe it is valid. Often they believe it is the only true one, or at least the highest one. These students will often say to, or about, messengers who come after their chosen organization that they cannot be valid. They will refer to something that was said in the old teaching or something that was said by the old messenger or in the popular culture of a certain organization, namely that this is the ultimate teaching and there will be nothing after it.

My beloved, why do you think we of the ascended masters began to express ourselves directly through messengers about a century ago? Why do you think we suddenly stepped out into the public awareness whereas in previous centuries we had been hidden? It was because there was an occult law that did not allow us to step out in the public view because humankind's consciousness had not risen to the necessary level. When that shift did occur and the consciousness was raised sufficiently, we were granted permission by the Karmic Board to express ourselves openly, and we immediately did so.

What were some of the first reactions we had? It was from orthodox religious people who said: "But why are you coming out with new revelation when our scripture has everything as the ultimate truth, has everything that was needed to be said?" We have heard Christians say this. We have heard Muslims. We have heard Jews. We have heard Buddhists, Hindus, Taoists, and every persuasion of spiritual movement. Why did we start expressing ourselves openly in the 1800s? Because we had more to say to humankind; we have a progressive, ongoing revelation. Yes, we have sponsored certain organizations and messengers. Yes, they have been valid while they were bringing forth new, progressive revelation, but then the dispensation ended for one reason or another.

Does that mean that we of the ascended masters now have nothing more to say? We have had ascended master students use the exact same logic as the orthodox religious people to argue against a messenger who came after their own. Do you think we want our students to go into the same mindset as orthodox or fundamentalist religious people? Do you think we want you to close your minds to our ongoing progressive revelation, clinging to a particular organization or messenger? We do not; we want you to move on when you are ready to move on.

This is not to say that you *have* to move on right now. Again, we are not seeking to get everyone to follow an ascended master teaching, and we are not seeking to get everyone to follow a specific ascended master teaching, including this one. It does mean that we want our students to be open to direction from within. If you get a direction to look beyond a particular outer teaching or to look at a new teaching, then we want you to follow that inner direction rather than deciding with your outer mind that: "Oh no, the masters could not possibly have anything more to say, for it has already been said in this previous teaching."

When you do this, you are failing to do what I said at the end of my last discourse. You are failing to let *us* be the masters, and you are failing to accept yourself as the student. You think you have become the master who can tell the ascended masters what they should or should not say, when they should or should not say it, and how they should or should not say it. This is not a constructive state of mind to be in if you want to rise beyond your current level of consciousness. It is certainly not a constructive state of mind to be in if you want to rise to the seventh level of the Second Ray and even rise beyond it and enter the initiations of the Third Ray.

Freedom in the Spirit of Wisdom

In order to rise to the seventh level and in order to pass the initiation on the seventh level, you need to be free when it comes to wisdom. This means, first of all, that you are free to move on when the Spirit of Wisdom moves you. You do not use the outer mind or a particular outer teaching to restrict, to limit, to put down, the Spirit of Wisdom. When you feel the inner urge to move, you move. You are constantly seeking to increase your attunement with the spirit. This is freedom; this is what we desire to see for our students. We are not hereby saying that you should decide with the outer mind to abandon an earlier teaching and move on to another one. We are saying you need to go beyond the outer mind and feel and know from within where the spirit moves you.

Freedom is one of the most difficult concepts for people to grasp, as Saint Germain has discoursed on several times. Freedom is the ultimate challenge, at least until you pass the initiations on the 96th level. Freedom is free; yet what do the ego and the false hierarchy impostors want? They want to say that freedom can only be free as defined by conditions on earth. This, of course, is not the case. You will not be truly free until you become one with the Spirit of Wisdom, and you will not become one with that spirit if you want to force it into a framework designed on earth. The spirit simply will not comply, and neither will the Spirit of Wisdom comply with your attempts to force it into a particular framework.

When you come to the seventh ray initiations in our retreat, you are, of course, not at the 96th level of consciousness. You are not expected to be at that level. You are not expected to be at the 144th level and be ready for your ascension. This means that there is absolutely no way you can grasp the highest wisdom. Whatever outer teaching you have come to accept at this point is the teaching you are able to grasp at your present level of consciousness and the teaching you found based on your outer situation, such as your culture and where you grew up. It is the best possible teaching for you right now, given your level of consciousness and your outer situation. We have no desire to have you forcefully get yourself to abandon a particular teaching or embrace another one.

What we actually desire to see is that you become free to embrace the teaching you have right now and to make the best possible use of it in order to grow further. We desire you to be free in embracing, studying, applying and living the teaching you have, the teaching you feel appeals to you in your present situation, whatever that teaching may be, be it an ascended master teaching, another religion or another spiritual teaching. Even if you have no teaching, we are not saying you should force yourself to adopt one. We want you to feel free in studying, internalizing and living the wisdom you have right now. You can only be truly free to study, internalize and apply a certain teaching if you do not seek to force yourself with the outer mind.

What it means to internalize a spiritual teaching

Do you remember what I said about the quantum leap that is necessary before a bird can push off from the nest and take flight for the first time? If you are seeking to force yourself from the linear mind to conform to a certain outer teaching or doctrine, a set of rules, or even a spiritual practice, then you are not free to let the spirit move you. This actually means that you will not be able to truly internalize and apply the teaching you have. If you will be honest and take a look at spiritual and religious movements, what is one of the main problems you see? It is precisely that so many people do not walk their talk. They have a certain teaching, they know, for example, that Jesus told them to turn the other cheek. It is one thing to have the teaching in the outer mind, it is another to apply it, to live it, in surprising situations. Many people feel they have grasped a certain teaching and they have become able to live according to it but then an unexpected situation happens, and now, suddenly, they are not able to apply the teaching. You will notice that I am not using irony or sarcasm here. I am just stating things plainly. I have no condemnation. I do not say this to provoke any kind of feeling of guilt or inadequacy in you. I say it because I wish you to see consciously that when you cannot walk your talk, when you cannot truly apply a certain teaching, it is because you have not been free to actually internalize the teaching. You have not been free because you are seeking with your outer mind to force your spirit to comply with an outer doctrine or set of rules.

Consider what it means to actually live a spiritual teaching. There are two ways to approach this. The approach taken by most people is that they seek to define an outer teaching, to define a certain set of rules for behavior, and then they seek with their outer minds to force themselves to conform to those rules. It is a matter of defining: "Do this, and don't do that." They think that if they comply with the outer behavior, then they are walking their talk, they are living their teaching. But why do you need an outer teaching?

As a person open to ascended master teachings you are open to the possibility that you can come to the point of ascending from earth. As I have just explained, the ascension is the ultimate quantum leap where you must throw off all the rules, restrictions, limitations and beliefs from earth. You must let go of *all* of them. If you are still seeking to force yourself to apply an outer set of rules, how could you possibly ascend? What we have attempted to explain, over and over again, is that the ascension is a process of coming into oneness with spirit, but how can you come into oneness through the outer mind that springs from the consciousness of separation? How can you solve a problem with the same state of consciousness that created the problem? How can you come into oneness through the consciousness of separation? How can the mortal self, the ego, bring you into the ascended state?

That is why I said that spiritual growth is not a linear process. It is not a matter of defining an outer set of rules and having to live up to it. It is a matter of coming to an inner realization, an inner recognition. What is the inner recognition you need to come to? So many spiritual people on earth believe that their particular teaching has defined an outer set of rules for what it takes to be worthy to enter the spiritual realm, the kingdom of heaven, the ascended state or however it is defined. This is not what a true teaching says. A true teaching says that when you have come into oneness with the spirit that you are, then you will *be* in the kingdom of heaven, for that spirit *is* the kingdom of heaven, and the kingdom is a state of oneness with spirit.

Your outer mind thinks it is a matter of living up to outer rules, but in reality it is a matter of freeing yourself from the outer restriction. It is a matter of realizing that you are what we have called the Conscious You, which is a formless being. You are not defined by any form on earth, and therefore you do not have to live up to any form on earth in order to enter the kingdom. You have to separate yourself from identification with any form and come into greater oneness with the spirit that you truly are.

How to live a spiritual teaching

What does it take to live up to a particular spiritual teaching? Take, for example, Jesus' call to turn the other cheek. How will you really, truly live up to this call and respond with non-violence whatever happens to you on earth? Can you see that you can never actually do this through the separate self? The separate self is separate, which means it feels threatened by things on earth. It *is* threatened by things on earth because the separate self is mortal and can be hurt by things on earth. Your I AM Presence exists in a higher realm. It does not feel threatened by any condition on earth because it knows it cannot be hurt by any condition on earth. Your I AM Presence has no problem at all living up to the call to turn the other cheek. It will turn the other cheek as an expression of its very nature.

We have given the teaching – and it is an important teaching – that the Conscious You exists in between the I AM Presence and the outer self. The real question is: How will the real you, the Conscious You, live up to the call of turning the other cheek? Can you do so by identifying with the outer self? You cannot, because the outer self can never actually live up to the call. What the outer self can do is that it can create a mental image that says: "You should not commit certain violent acts." Then you can seek to force yourself to live up to that image by not committing these acts, and you may be successful in doing this if you are not exposed to conditions that shock you out of your sense of equilibrium.

Many Christians, for example, are able to be non-violent, peaceful and calm as long as they are in situations where they feel they have everything under control. Put them in a situation that shocks them, and you will see that they will begin to falter in their resolve to turn the other cheek. There can easily come a situation when they cannot walk their talk anymore because the situation is too different from what they feel they can control. The outer mind seeks to achieve something through control, but as we have said, everything you do on earth becomes an energy impulse that is sent into the cosmic mirror and the cosmic mirror will reflect it back multiplied.

By the very fact that you are seeking to attain non-violence through control, you are sending an energy impulse which will be returned to you by the mirror as circumstances that are more intense than your current situation. It is just a matter of time before what comes back to you from the mirror is more intense than what you can control with the outer mind—and you lapse out of your resolve to turn the other cheek. You take some kind of violent action and then, of course, the ego and the false hierarchy impostors are right there, now wanting you to feel guilty for the fact that you could not walk your talk. Then, you are in this downward spiral of seeking to justify yourself and seeking to control yourself even more, and it ends up becoming such a strain that people sooner or later will have to throw in the towel and say: "I just can't do this anymore."

We would rather see our students come to the realization that there is a better way, and the better way is that you realize that you are the Conscious You. You have the option of withdrawing yourself from identification with the outer mind, the separate self. Instead, you can come into oneness with the I AM Presence. Now you are not being non-violent because you are forcing yourself to comply with an outer idea; you are allowing the Presence to express itself through you, and the Presence is by nature non-violent.

That is how you walk your talk. *That* is how you live your teaching, by allowing the Conscious You to disentangle itself from identification with the outer self, shifting your sense of identity into identification with the I AM Presence. You are becoming the open door for the I AM Presence to express itself through you, and that is really the only way that you can walk your talk and fully integrate, internalize and express a spiritual teaching. You are not seeking to express the outer spiritual teaching.

Your goal is not to know and comply with an outer set of rules. Your goal is to use a spiritual teaching only as a ladder for climbing towards oneness with the spirit, and then you allow the spirit to express itself through you.

Climb towards oneness with the spirit

We realize fully that at this level of initiation, you cannot do this to the full extent. We are not asking this from you. What we are asking is that you consider these teachings, even with the conscious mind, and you consider what it would take for you to make a quantum leap in your conscious awareness to where you shift your focus away from seeking to comply with an outer teaching. Instead, you shift your focus into seeking first the kingdom of God whereby all other things shall be added onto you because you seek oneness with the spirit. You make this your outer, conscious goal.

I realize that you cannot instantly jump into total oneness with the spirit, but when you come to the seventh level of initiation under the Second Ray, you can realize that the superior wisdom is not that you apply a spiritual teaching the way it has been done by so many people in the past. The higher wisdom you can step up to is that you realize that the goal of a spiritual teaching is to come into oneness with the spirit behind the teaching. When you make this your goal, you will be so much more free. You do not have to force yourself to comply with a linear interpretation of the outer teaching and its rules. You will be surprised at how much lighter you will feel when you no longer have to force yourself, not only your outer behavior but your thoughts and feelings.

The difference between true and false teachings

Have you ever actually stepped back and looked at yourself and how you are using a spiritual teaching to force your thoughts and feelings and your behavior into certain patterns defined by the teaching? Have you allowed yourself to actually feel how much of a strain this is upon you? I know very well what the outer self, the false hierarchy impostors and many other people will say about this teaching. They will say: "It *must* be a false teaching, for have not the teachings said that if you are constant in your application of this or that teaching, you will surely make it to the ultimate goal?" That is not actually what the teaching is saying—unless it is a false teaching.

What a true ascended master teaching is saying is that if you are constant in always seeking to transcend your current level of consciousness, then you will qualify for your ascension. This is all that a true spiritual teaching *can* say. A true teaching cannot promise you that, by following outer rules and rituals or believing in a certain outer teaching, you will *automatically* qualify for your ascension. A true teaching can only be given from the ascended level, and a being who has ascended knows what it takes to ascend. This being knows that in the end you must transcend all outer teachings, all worded beliefs and images.

You must let them all go and come into oneness with the spirit that cannot be captured in words. The spirit can be expressed through words, but it cannot be confined to any particular expression. It is always more than can be expressed through words, and you only come into oneness with the spirit by reaching for the more that is beyond the words. When you fix your outer attention on the words, then you are essentially saying to the spirit: "Leave me alone for I want to feel superior in my application of this outer teaching." It is your right to make this decision. I can only champion your right, but I will also say that then you have lost the Spirit of Wisdom that I AM.

You cannot be my student if you reject the spirit that I AM. I AM Lanto. I am the Chohan of the Second Ray. I can express myself through words, as I have done in this book. I AM *in* the words, but I am *more* than the words. If you think you can take this book and study it, and study it, and study it and apply the tools and then you will come into oneness with the spirit, then you are mistaken. You will come into oneness with me only by transcending the outer teaching and tools. You use the teaching and the tools to tune in to the spirit. What so many religious people have done over the ages is to set up an outer teaching, define it as superior, and then they seek to force God – they seek to force the spirit – to comply with and validate the outer teaching. This is, again, the separate self seeking to force everything. What chance do you think the ego and the separate self has of forcing the spirit into a certain matrix? There are many, many people on earth who actually believe in the lies spread by the fallen beings that it is possible to force the spirit to comply. The fallen beings have believed for a long time that they can, one day, build such a pressure that they force God to comply with their definition of God.

When you come to the seventh level in the Royal Teton Retreat, you are at the point where you are able to make a quantum leap and experience the fallacy of this approach. You are able to see that the Spirit of Wisdom will never comply with an outer teaching expressed in words. It will always be more, and you will know the spirit only by going beyond the words and coming into oneness with the spirit. This you are able to know. You are able to know this with the conscious mind and when you know this, you can be free.

Whatever teaching applies to you at your present level, embrace the teaching. Study it, practice it, but, first of all, strive to internalize it and strive to use the outer teaching to reach for the spirit that is beyond the teaching. If you will do this, any outer teaching will take you higher. It will take you to the highest point on the path that the teaching can take you. If you then still strive for oneness with the spirit, you will get the inner direction of where to go next, whether it be another outer teaching or whether you are ready to go within and establish your own inner contact with your Christ Self, I AM Presence and ascended teachers.

A combination of linear steps and quantum leaps

At the Royal Teton Retreat, I have created a special room where I will take the students who have begun to grasp the initiation on the seventh level. I will not do this before they have actually grasped the initiation, but after. I will, as a reward, take them in there and show them how planet earth can be pictured as a beautiful tapestry. It is almost like a map, and it shows that there is a goal that you need to reach. It is almost like a mountain, and then the tapestry shows how there are many different routes that lead towards the mountain. It also shows that there is no route that leads directly to the mountain, for every route has certain stages where you must cross a chasm, a divide of some kind.

Most of the journey you are walking, but there are certain points where you cannot cross to the other side by walking. There may be a river. There may be a deep gorge. There may be a swamp or a dense forest. But you cannot cross by walking. You must find another way. You must take the quantum leap, as I have shown. You can get far by walking, but if you come to a river, walking is not going to do you much good. You need another mode of transportation. You need a boat, or you may come to a deep gorge where you need a bridge or a rope that you can slide across.

My point is that students at this level can see that the path is not linear; it is a combination of linear steps and quantum leaps. There is a time where you walk through a series of linear steps, but then there comes the point where you take a quantum leap to the other side. If you do not make the quantum leap but keep walking, you end up walking in circles, as you know very well that people who walk in the desert and have no landmarks end up walking in circles.

When students see this tapestry, they often become very excited. They see the intense beauty of the path. They see that, behind all the outer conditions they have faced, there is this beautiful path that leads everyone home. So many students have faced very difficult conditions in their outer lives, but when they come to this level of my retreat, I can show them that no matter how ugly, unspiritual or unpleasant the conditions have been, they can all be turned into stepping stones for moving forward on the path. They can all be used to propel yourself higher when you transcend the outer situation and reach for the spirit behind it.

The spirit is always behind everything. The lie of the outer self, the lie of the false teachers, is that there are conditions on earth that are so ugly, so humiliating, so degrading, so inhumane, so unspiritual that you cannot reach for the spirit in those situations. In terms of wisdom, the false hierarchy will want you to believe that you have to comply with an outer expression of wisdom, and therefore you cannot ever reach for the Spirit of Wisdom. All you need is the outer wisdom, and that will take you to the ultimate destination. When you see this is just a blind alley and it has no reality, then the student is free to embrace wisdom in a particular form but realize that the real goal is to reach for the spirit. Whatever the outer situation, whatever the outer form or expression of wisdom, the real goal is to reach for the spirit.

Moving on to the initiations of the Third Ray

When you realize this, then you are free to flow with the Spirit of Wisdom. Then, I will take you on a journey where you, for a certain interval, experience what it is like to flow with the Spirit of Wisdom. This journey will not be so long, for we are not taking this ride in order to just enjoy flowing with wisdom. We are actually taking this ride to cross the chasm that leads you from the initiations of the Second Ray to the initiations of the Third Ray and my beloved brother, Paul the Venetian, who is waiting for you at the Chateau de Liberty. He will then take you through the initiations, the seven levels of initiation, under the Third Ray of God Love.

It is a great joy for me when a student is ready. You may think that I would want to keep the students that have passed all levels of initiations in my retreat. This would be a human way of thinking. You may think with the human mind that it is my goal as the master of the Second Ray retreat to raise students up to pass all initiations under my retreat, and then I would want to enjoy the spoils of my labor. I would want to parade my best students and feel proud over having taken them this far. This is what a false teacher would do, but I am not a false teacher. I am a true teacher.

My only purpose for teaching a student is to take that student as far as I am meant to take that student and then help the student move on to the next level of initiation. It is not in seeing the student pass some ultimate level of initiation that I get my ultimate joy and fulfillment. It is in seeing the student move on and seeing that student be greeted by Paul the Venetian. *That* is my supreme joy. I know that after you reach the 96th level of initiation, you can easily come back to me if you so choose, but I have no need and no desire to own anyone or anything, *for I am free!*

I am not only flowing with the Spirit of Wisdom, *I AM* the Spirit of Wisdom. That may sound like a meaningless distinction at your present level of consciousness, but before you make your ascension from this earth, you will know the full meaning of what I just said. You will realize that you, too, *are* the Spirit of Wisdom and the spirits of the other six God qualities. You will even know that you are a spirit that is beyond the rays but is a combination of all of the rays—but is still more than this, for the rays have form, but the spirit is beyond form.

So am I, even though I take on a certain form so that you have something that you can grasp with your present level of awareness. But do not think I can be confined to the form I have taken on. Although I am not Master MORE, I am both a master and I AM *more*. I AM Lanto, Lord of the Second Ray! But I am more than the Chohan, for I am the ineffable spirit. When you know, when you experience, your own ineffability, then you will know *me*.

17 | I INVOKE FREEDOM IN THE SPIRIT

In the name I AM THAT I AM, Jesus Christ, I call to my I AM Presence to flow through the I Will Be Presence that I AM and give this invocation with full power. I call to beloved Elohim Apollo and Lumina and Arcturus and Victoria, Archangel Jophiel and Christine and Zadkiel and Amethyst, Master Lanto and Saint Germain to help me use any experience on earth to transcend the outer form and come into oneness with the spirit behind everything. Help me see and surrender all patterns that block my oneness with Master Lanto and my oneness with my I AM Presence, including …

[Make personal calls]

1. I meet the challenge of freedom

1. I am an ascended master student and it is my goal to climb from the 48th to the 96th level of consciousness. I surrender the desire to define an ultimate truth and I am free in expressing wisdom without having to compare it to something defined with words.

Beloved Apollo, with your second ray,
you open my eyes to see a new day,
I see through duality's lies and deceit,
transcending the mindset producing defeat.

**Beloved Apollo, thou Elohim Gold,
your radiant light my eyes now behold,
as pages of wisdom you gently unfold,
I feel I am free from all that is old.**

2. I am stepping outside the perception filter of the outer self and experiencing the Spirit of Wisdom. I surrender all limited vision and all tendency to set myself up as the judge of others.

Beloved Apollo, in your flame I know,
that your living wisdom is always a flow,
in your light I see my own highest will,
immersed in the stream that never stands still.

**Beloved Apollo, your light makes it clear,
why we have taken embodiment here,
working to raise our own cosmic sphere,
together we form the tip of the spear.**

3. I cannot know with the outer mind what the Spirit of Wisdom desires to express through me in a particular situation. I am giving room for the Spirit of Wisdom to express itself through me freely.

Beloved Apollo, exposing all lies,
I hereby surrender all ego-based ties,
I know my perception is truly the key,
to transcending the serpentine duality.

> **Beloved Apollo, we heed now your call,**
> **drawing us into Wisdom's Great Hall,**
> **exposing all lies causing the fall,**
> **you help us reclaim the oneness of all.**

4. I am following my inner direction to look beyond a particular outer teaching or to look at a new teaching. I am letting the ascended masters be the masters, and I accept myself as the student. I am flowing with the ongoing progressive revelation of the ascended masters.

> Beloved Apollo, your wisdom so clear,
> in oneness with you, no serpent I fear,
> the beam in my eye I'm willing to see,
> I'm free from the serpent's own duality.

> **Beloved Apollo, my eyes now I raise,**
> **I see that the Earth is in a new phase,**
> **I willingly stand in your piercing gaze,**
> **empowered, I exit duality's maze.**

5. I am rising beyond my current level of consciousness. I am rising to the seventh level of the Second Ray and I am free to move on when the Spirit of Wisdom moves me.

> Beloved Arcturus, release now the flow,
> of Violet Flame to help all life grow,
> in ever-expanding circles of Light,
> it pulses within every atom so bright.

> **Beloved Arcturus, thou Elohim Free,**
> **I open my heart to your reality,**
> **expanding my heart into Infinity,**
> **your flame is the key to my God-victory.**

6. I do not use the outer mind or a particular outer teaching to restrict the Spirit of Wisdom. When I feel the inner urge to move, I move. I am constantly increasing my attunement with the spirit. This is freedom; this is what the ascended masters desire to see for their students.

> Beloved Arcturus, be with me alway,
> reborn, I am ready to face a new day,
> I have no attachments to life here on Earth,
> I claim a new life in your Flame of Rebirth.
>
> **Beloved Arcturus, your Violet Flame pure,**
> **is for every ailment the ultimate cure,**
> **against it no darkness could ever endure,**
> **my freedom it will forever ensure.**

7. Freedom is the ultimate challenge. Freedom is free; yet the ego and the false hierarchy impostors want me to say that freedom can only be free as defined by conditions on earth.

> Beloved Arcturus, your bright violet fire,
> now fills every atom, raising them higher,
> the space in each atom all filled with your light,
> as matter itself is shining so bright.
>
> **Beloved Arcturus, your transforming Grace,**
> **empowers me now every challenge to face,**
> **as your violet light floods my inner space,**
> **towards my ascension I willingly race.**

8. I will not be truly free until I become one with the Spirit of Wisdom, and I will not become one with that spirit if I want to force it into a framework designed on earth. The Spirit of Wisdom will *not* comply with my attempts to force it into a particular framework.

> Beloved Arcturus, bring in a new age,
> help Earth and humanity turn a new page,
> your transforming light gives me certainty,
> Saint Germain's Golden Age is a reality.

> **Beloved Arcturus, I surrender all fear,**
> **I AM feeling your Presence so tangibly near,**
> **with your Freedom's Song filling my ear,**
> **I know that to God I AM ever so dear.**

9. Master Lanto, help me accept that the outer teaching I have at this point is the best possible teaching for me right now, given my level of consciousness and my outer situation.

> Accelerate my Awakeness, I AM real,
> Accelerate my Awakeness, all life heal,
> Accelerate my Awakeness, I AM MORE,
> Accelerate my Awakeness, all will soar.

> Accelerate my Awakeness! (3X)
> Beloved Apollo and Lumina.
> Accelerate my Awakeness! (3X)
> Beloved Jophiel and Christine.
> Accelerate my Awakeness! (3X)
> Beloved Master Lanto.
> Accelerate my Awakeness! (3X)
> Beloved I AM.

2. I am not defined by anything on earth

1. Master Lanto, help me embrace the teaching I have right now and make the best possible use of it in order to grow further. Help me be free in embracing, studying, applying and living the teaching that appeals to me in my present situation.

> Jophiel Archangel, in wisdom's great light,
> all serpentine lies exposed to my sight.
> So subtle the lies that creep through the mind,
> yet you are the greatest teacher I find.

Jophiel Archangel, exposing all lies,
Jophiel Archangel, cutting all ties.
Jophiel Archangel, clearing the skies,
Jophiel Archangel, my mind truly flies.

2. I am free in studying, internalizing and living the wisdom I have right now. I am truly free because I do not seek to force myself with the outer mind.

> Jophiel Archangel, your wisdom I hail,
> your sword cutting through duality's veil.
> As you show the way, I know what is real,
> from serpentine doubt, I instantly heal.

Jophiel Archangel, exposing all lies,
Jophiel Archangel, cutting all ties.
Jophiel Archangel, clearing the skies,
Jophiel Archangel, my mind truly flies.

3. I surrender the desire to force myself to conform to a set of rules, and I am free to let the spirit move me. I am able to truly internalize and apply the teaching I have. I am walking my talk.

17 | I Invoke Freedom in the Spirit

Jophiel Archangel, your reality,
the best antidote to duality.
No lie can remain in your Presence so clear,
with you on my side, no serpent I fear.

Jophiel Archangel, exposing all lies,
Jophiel Archangel, cutting all ties.
Jophiel Archangel, clearing the skies,
Jophiel Archangel, my mind truly flies.

4. I am open to the possibility that I can come to the point of ascending from earth. The ascension is the ultimate quantum leap where I must throw off all the rules, restrictions, limitations and beliefs from earth. I must let go of *all* of them.

Jophiel Archangel, God's mind is in me,
and through your clear light, its wisdom I see.
Divisions all vanish, as I see the One,
and truly, the wholeness of mind I have won.

Jophiel Archangel, exposing all lies,
Jophiel Archangel, cutting all ties.
Jophiel Archangel, clearing the skies,
Jophiel Archangel, my mind truly flies.

5. The ascension is a process of coming into oneness with spirit, but I cannot come into oneness through the outer mind that springs from the consciousness of separation. The mortal self, the ego, cannot bring me into the ascended state.

Zadkiel Archangel, your flow is so swift,
in your violet light, I instantly shift,
into a vibration in which I am free,
from all limitations of the lesser me.

**Zadkiel Archangel, encircle the earth,
Zadkiel Archangel, with your violet girth,
Zadkiel Archangel, unstoppable mirth,
Zadkiel Archangel, our planet's rebirth.**

6. Spiritual growth is not a linear process. It is not a matter of defining an outer set of rules and living up to them. It is a matter of coming to an inner realization, an inner recognition.

Zadkiel Archangel, I truly aspire,
to being the master of your violet fire.
Wielding the power, of your alchemy,
I use Sacred Word, to set all life free.

**Zadkiel Archangel, encircle the earth,
Zadkiel Archangel, with your violet girth,
Zadkiel Archangel, unstoppable mirth,
Zadkiel Archangel, our planet's rebirth.**

7. When I have come into oneness with the spirit that I AM, then I will *be* in the kingdom of heaven, for that spirit *is* the kingdom of heaven, and the kingdom is a state of oneness with spirit.

Zadkiel Archangel, your violet light,
transforming the earth, with unstoppable might.
So swiftly our planet, beginning to spin,
with legions of angels, our victory we win.

**Zadkiel Archangel, encircle the earth,
Zadkiel Archangel, with your violet girth,
Zadkiel Archangel, unstoppable mirth,
Zadkiel Archangel, our planet's rebirth.**

8. This is a matter of freeing myself from the outer restriction. It is a matter of realizing that I am the Conscious You, which is a formless being.

> Zadkiel Archangel, your violet flame,
> the earth and humanity, never the same.
> Saint Germain's Golden Age, is a reality,
> what glorious wonder, I joyously see.
>
> **Zadkiel Archangel, encircle the earth,**
> **Zadkiel Archangel, with your violet girth,**
> **Zadkiel Archangel, unstoppable mirth,**
> **Zadkiel Archangel, our planet's rebirth.**

9. I am not defined by any form on earth, and therefore I do not have to live up to any form on earth in order to enter the kingdom. I have to separate myself from identification with any form and come into greater oneness with the spirit that I AM.

> With angels I soar,
> as I reach for MORE.
> The angels so real,
> their love all will heal.
> The angels bring peace,
> all conflicts will cease.
> With angels of light,
> we soar to new height.
>
> **The rustling sound of angel wings,**
> **what joy as even matter sings,**
> **what joy as every atom rings,**
> **in harmony with angel wings.**

3. I am living my spiritual teaching

1. How can I truly turn the other cheek? The separate self is separate, which means it feels threatened by things on earth. It *is* threatened by things on earth because the separate self is mortal and can be hurt by things on earth.

> Master Lanto, golden wise,
> expose in me the ego's lies.
> Master Lanto, will to be,
> I will to win my mastery.
>
> **O Holy Spirit, flow through me,**
> **I am the open door for thee.**
> **O mighty rushing stream of Light,**
> **transcendence is my sacred right.**

2. My I AM Presence exists in a higher realm. It does not feel threatened by any condition on earth because it knows it cannot be hurt by any condition on earth. My I AM Presence will turn the other cheek as an expression of its very nature.

> Master Lanto, balance all,
> for wisdom's balance I do call.
> Master Lanto, help me see,
> that balance is the Golden key.
>
> **O Holy Spirit, flow through me,**
> **I am the open door for thee.**
> **O mighty rushing stream of Light,**
> **transcendence is my sacred right.**

3. The Conscious You exists in between the I AM Presence and the outer self. The outer mind seeks to achieve something through control, but this creates an energy impulse that will threaten my sense of control when returned by the cosmic mirror.

> Master Lanto, from Above,
> I call forth discerning love.
> Master Lanto, love's not blind,
> through love, God vision I will find.
>
> **O Holy Spirit, flow through me,**
> **I am the open door for thee.**
> **O mighty rushing stream of Light,**
> **transcendence is my sacred right.**

4. The better way is to realize that I am the Conscious You. I am withdrawing myself from identification with the outer mind, the separate self. I am in oneness with my I AM Presence. I am allowing the Presence to express itself through me, and the Presence is by nature non-violent.

> Master Lanto, pure I am,
> intentions pure as Christic lamb.
> Master Lanto, I will transcend,
> acceleration now my truest friend.
>
> **O Holy Spirit, flow through me,**
> **I am the open door for thee.**
> **O mighty rushing stream of Light,**
> **transcendence is my sacred right.**

5. I am living my teaching by allowing the Conscious You to disentangle itself from identification with the outer self. I am shifting my sense of identity into identification with the I AM Presence. I am the open door for the I AM Presence to express itself through me.

> Master Lanto, I am whole,
> no more division in my soul.
> Master Lanto, healing flame,
> all balance in your sacred name.

> **O Holy Spirit, flow through me,**
> **I am the open door for thee.**
> **O mighty rushing stream of Light,**
> **transcendence is my sacred right.**

6. I am fully integrating, internalizing and expressing my spiritual teaching. My goal is to use the spiritual teaching only as a ladder for climbing towards oneness with the spirit, and then I allow the spirit to express itself through me.

> Master Lanto, serve all life,
> as I transcend all inner strife.
> Master Lanto, peace you give,
> to all who want to truly live.

> **O Holy Spirit, flow through me,**
> **I am the open door for thee.**
> **O mighty rushing stream of Light,**
> **transcendence is my sacred right.**

7. Master Lanto, help me make a quantum leap in my conscious awareness to where I shift my focus away from seeking to comply with an outer teaching. I shift my focus into seeking first the kingdom of God whereby all other things shall be added onto me because I seek oneness with the spirit. I hereby make this my outer, conscious goal.

> Master Lanto, free to be,
> in balanced creativity.
> Master Lanto, we employ,
> your balance as the key to joy.

> **O Holy Spirit, flow through me,**
> **I am the open door for thee.**
> **O mighty rushing stream of Light,**
> **transcendence is my sacred right.**

8. Master Lanto, help me realize that the superior wisdom is not that I apply a spiritual teaching the way it has been done by so many people in the past. The higher wisdom is that the goal of a spiritual teaching is to come into oneness with the spirit behind the teaching.

> Master Lanto, balance all,
> the seven rays upon my call.
> Master Lanto, I take flight,
> my threefold flame a blazing light.

> **O Holy Spirit, flow through me,**
> **I am the open door for thee.**
> **O mighty rushing stream of Light,**
> **transcendence is my sacred right.**

9. I hereby make this my goal, and I am free. I do not have to force myself to comply with a linear interpretation of the outer teaching and its rules. I am feeling much lighter because I no longer have to force my outer behavior or my thoughts and feelings.

> Lanto dear, your Presence here,
> filling up my inner sphere.
> Life is now a sacred flow,
> God Wisdom I on all bestow.

**O Holy Spirit, flow through me,
I am the open door for thee.
O mighty rushing stream of Light,
transcendence is my sacred right.**

4. I am free in flowing with the spirit that I AM

1. Master Lanto, I see that I cannot be your student if I reject the spirit that you are. You can express yourself through words, but you are *more* than the words. I am coming into oneness with you by transcending the outer teaching, using it to tune in to the spirit.

> Saint Germain, your alchemy,
> with violet fire now sets me free.
> Saint Germain, I ever grow,
> in freedom's overpowering flow.

**O Holy Spirit, flow through me,
I am the open door for thee.
O mighty rushing stream of Light,
transcendence is my sacred right.**

2. I am surrendering the desire to force God, to force the spirit, to comply with and validate the outer teaching. This is the separate self seeking to force everything.

> Saint Germain, your mastery,
> of violet flame geometry.
> Saint Germain, in you I see,
> the formulas that set me free.

> **O Holy Spirit, flow through me,**
> **I am the open door for thee.**
> **O mighty rushing stream of Light,**
> **transcendence is my sacred right.**

3. Master Lanto, help me see through and surrender the lie spread by the fallen beings that it is possible to force the spirit to comply with any teaching on earth. I am making a quantum leap and experiencing the fallacy of this approach.

> Saint Germain, in Liberty,
> I feel the love you have for me.
> Saint Germain, I do adore,
> the violet flame that makes all more.

> **O Holy Spirit, flow through me,**
> **I am the open door for thee.**
> **O mighty rushing stream of Light,**
> **transcendence is my sacred right.**

4. The Spirit of Wisdom will never comply with an outer teaching expressed in words. It will always be more, and I will know the spirit only by going beyond the words and coming into oneness with the spirit. In knowing this, I am free.

> Saint Germain, in unity,
> I will transcend duality.
> Saint Germain, my self so pure,
> your violet chemistry so sure.
>
> **O Holy Spirit, flow through me,
> I am the open door for thee.
> O mighty rushing stream of Light,
> transcendence is my sacred right.**

5. Master Lanto, help me see that the path is not linear; it is a combination of linear steps and quantum leaps. There is a time where I walk through a series of linear steps, but then there comes the point where I make a quantum leap beyond my current level.

> Saint Germain, reality,
> in violet light I am carefree.
> Saint Germain, my aura seal,
> your violet flame my chakras heal.
>
> **O Holy Spirit, flow through me,
> I am the open door for thee.
> O mighty rushing stream of Light,
> transcendence is my sacred right.**

6. Master Lanto, help me see that even the most ugly, unspiritual or unpleasant conditions can be turned into stepping stones for moving forward on the path. I am using all of my experiences to propel myself higher by transcending the outer situation and reaching for the spirit behind it.

Saint Germain, your chemistry,
with violet fire set atoms free.
Saint Germain, from lead to gold,
transforming vision I behold.

**O Holy Spirit, flow through me,
I am the open door for thee.
O mighty rushing stream of Light,
transcendence is my sacred right.**

7. The spirit is always behind everything. The lie of the outer self, the lie of the false teachers, is that there are conditions on earth that are so ugly, so humiliating, so degrading, so inhumane, so unspiritual that I cannot reach for the Spirit of Wisdom in those situations.

Saint Germain, transcendency,
as I am always one with thee.
Saint Germain, from soul I'm free,
I so delight in being me.

**O Holy Spirit, flow through me,
I am the open door for thee.
O mighty rushing stream of Light,
transcendence is my sacred right.**

8. I am free to embrace wisdom in a particular form, but I realize that the real goal is to reach for the spirit. I am free to flow with the Spirit of Wisdom. Master Lanto, take me on a journey where I experience what it is like to flow with the Spirit of Wisdom.

> Saint Germain, nobility,
> the key to sacred alchemy.
> Saint Germain, you balance all,
> the seven rays upon my call.
>
> **O Holy Spirit, flow through me,
> I am the open door for thee.
> O mighty rushing stream of Light,
> transcendence is my sacred right.**

9. Master Lanto, help me realize that I, too, *am* the Spirit of Wisdom and the spirits of the other six God qualities. Help me know that I am a spirit that is beyond the rays but is a combination of all of the rays. I AM still more than this, for the rays have form, but the spirit is beyond form.

> Saint Germain, your Presence here,
> filling up my inner sphere.
> Life is now a sacred flow,
> God Freedom I on all bestow.
>
> **O Holy Spirit, flow through me,
> I am the open door for thee.
> O mighty rushing stream of Light,
> transcendence is my sacred right.**

Sealing:

In the name of the Divine Mother, I fully accept that the power of these calls is used to set free the Ma-ter light, so it can outpicture the perfect vision of Christ for my own life, for all people and for the planet. In the name I AM THAT I AM, it is done! Amen.

2.01: DECREE TO APOLLO AND LUMINA

In the name I AM THAT I AM, Jesus Christ, I call to my I Will Be Presence to flow through my being and give these decrees with full power. I call to beloved Mighty Apollo and Lumina to release flood tides of Wisdom's Golden Light to help us see through the most subtle deceptions of dualistic forces, including…

[Make personal calls]

1. Beloved Apollo, with your second ray,
you open my eyes to see a new day,
I see through duality's lies and deceit,
transcending the mindset producing defeat.

**Beloved Apollo, thou Elohim Gold,
your radiant light my eyes now behold,
as pages of wisdom you gently unfold,
I feel I am free from all that is old.**

2. Beloved Apollo, in your flame I know,
that your living wisdom is always a flow,
in your light I see my own highest will,
immersed in the stream that never stands still.

**Beloved Apollo, your light makes it clear,
why we have taken embodiment here,
working to raise our own cosmic sphere,
together we form the tip of the spear.**

3. Beloved Apollo, exposing all lies,
I hereby surrender all ego-based ties,
I know my perception is truly the key,
to transcending the serpentine duality.

**Beloved Apollo, we heed now your call,
drawing us into Wisdom's Great Hall,
exposing all lies causing the fall,
you help us reclaim the oneness of all.**

4. Beloved Apollo, your wisdom so clear,
in oneness with you, no serpent I fear,
the beam in my eye I'm willing to see,
I'm free from the serpent's own duality.

**Beloved Apollo, my eyes now I raise,
I see that the Earth is in a new phase,
I willingly stand in your piercing gaze,
empowered, I exit duality's maze.**

Coda:
Accelerate my Awakeness, I AM real,
Accelerate my Awakeness, all life heal,
Accelerate my Awakeness, I AM MORE,
Accelerate my Awakeness, all will soar.

Accelerate my Awakeness! (3X)
Beloved Apollo and Lumina.
Accelerate my Awakeness! (3X)
Beloved Jophiel and Christine.
Accelerate my Awakeness! (3X)
Beloved Master Lanto.
Accelerate my Awakeness! (3X)
Beloved I AM.

Sealing:

In the name of the Divine Mother, I fully accept that the power of these calls is used to set free the Ma-ter light, so it can outpicture the perfect vision of Christ for my own life, for all people and for the planet. In the name I AM THAT I AM, it is done! Amen.

2.02: DECREE TO ARCHANGEL JOPHIEL

In the name I AM THAT I AM, Jesus Christ, I call to my I AM Presence to flow through the I Will Be Presence that I AM and give these decrees with full power. I call to beloved Archangel Jophiel and Christine to shield me in your wings of golden yellow light, and shatter and consume all serpentine lies and dualistic illusions, including…

[Make personal calls]

1. Jophiel Archangel, in wisdom's great light,
all serpentine lies exposed to my sight.
So subtle the lies that creep through the mind,
yet you are the greatest teacher I find.

Jophiel Archangel, exposing all lies,
Jophiel Archangel, cutting all ties.
Jophiel Archangel, clearing the skies,
Jophiel Archangel, my mind truly flies.

2. Jophiel Archangel, your wisdom I hail,
your sword cutting through duality's veil.
As you show the way, I know what is real,
from serpentine doubt, I instantly heal.

**Jophiel Archangel, exposing all lies,
Jophiel Archangel, cutting all ties.
Jophiel Archangel, clearing the skies,
Jophiel Archangel, my mind truly flies.**

3. Jophiel Archangel, your reality,
the best antidote to duality.
No lie can remain in your Presence so clear,
with you on my side, no serpent I fear.

**Jophiel Archangel, exposing all lies,
Jophiel Archangel, cutting all ties.
Jophiel Archangel, clearing the skies,
Jophiel Archangel, my mind truly flies.**

4. Jophiel Archangel, God's mind is in me,
and through your clear light, its wisdom I see.
Divisions all vanish, as I see the One,
and truly, the wholeness of mind I have won.

**Jophiel Archangel, exposing all lies,
Jophiel Archangel, cutting all ties.
Jophiel Archangel, clearing the skies,
Jophiel Archangel, my mind truly flies.**

Coda:
With angels I soar,
as I reach for MORE.
The angels so real,
their love all will heal.
The angels bring peace,
all conflicts will cease.
With angels of light,
we soar to new height.

The rustling sound of angel wings,
what joy as even matter sings,
what joy as every atom rings,
in harmony with angel wings.

Sealing:

In the name of the Divine Mother, I fully accept that the power of these calls is used to set free the Ma-ter light, so it can outpicture the perfect vision of Christ for my own life, for all people and for the planet. In the name I AM THAT I AM, it is done! Amen.

2.03: DECREE TO MASTER LANTO

In the name I AM THAT I AM, Jesus Christ, I call to my I AM Presence to flow through the I Will Be Presence that I AM and give these decrees with full power. I call to beloved Master Lanto, the other Chohans and the Maha Chohan to release flood tides of light, to consume all blocks and attachments that prevent me from becoming one with the eternal flow of the second ray of creative wisdom and ever-transcending reality, including…

[Make personal calls]

1. Master Lanto, golden wise,
expose in me the ego's lies.
Master Lanto, will to be,
I will to win my mastery.

**O Holy Spirit, flow through me,
I am the open door for thee.
O mighty rushing stream of Light,
transcendence is my sacred right.**

2. Master Lanto, balance all,
for wisdom's balance I do call.
Master Lanto, help me see,
that balance is the Golden key.

**O Holy Spirit, flow through me,
I am the open door for thee.
O mighty rushing stream of Light,
transcendence is my sacred right.**

3. Master Lanto, from Above,
I call forth discerning love.
Master Lanto, love's not blind,
through love, God vision I will find.

**O Holy Spirit, flow through me,
I am the open door for thee.
O mighty rushing stream of Light,
transcendence is my sacred right.**

4. Master Lanto, pure I am,
intentions pure as Christic lamb.
Master Lanto, I will transcend,
acceleration now my truest friend.

**O Holy Spirit, flow through me,
I am the open door for thee.
O mighty rushing stream of Light,
transcendence is my sacred right.**

5. Master Lanto, I am whole,
no more division in my soul.
Master Lanto, healing flame,
all balance in your sacred name.

**O Holy Spirit, flow through me,
I am the open door for thee.
O mighty rushing stream of Light,
transcendence is my sacred right.**

6. Master Lanto, serve all life,
as I transcend all inner strife.
Master Lanto, peace you give,
to all who want to truly live.

**O Holy Spirit, flow through me,
I am the open door for thee.
O mighty rushing stream of Light,
transcendence is my sacred right.**

7. Master Lanto, free to be,
in balanced creativity.
Master Lanto, we employ,
your balance as the key to joy.

**O Holy Spirit, flow through me,
I am the open door for thee.
O mighty rushing stream of Light,
transcendence is my sacred right.**

8. Master Lanto, balance all,
the seven rays upon my call.
Master Lanto, I take flight,
my threefold flame a blazing light.

**O Holy Spirit, flow through me,
I am the open door for thee.
O mighty rushing stream of Light,
transcendence is my sacred right.**

9. Lanto dear, your Presence here,
filling up my inner sphere.
Life is now a sacred flow,
God Wisdom I on all bestow.

**O Holy Spirit, flow through me,
I am the open door for thee.
O mighty rushing stream of Light,
transcendence is my sacred right.**

Sealing:

In the name of the Divine Mother, I fully accept that the power of these calls is used to set free the Ma-ter light, so it can outpicture the perfect vision of Christ for my own life, for all people and for the planet. In the name I AM THAT I AM, it is done! Amen.

About the Author

Kim Michaels is a prolific author, having published over 40 books. He has conducted spiritual conferences and workshops in 14 countries, has counseled hundreds of spiritual students and has done numerous radio shows on spiritual topics. Kim has been on the spiritual path since 1976. He has studied a wide variety of spiritual teachings and practiced many techniques for raising consciousness. Since 2002 he has served as a messenger for Jesus and other ascended masters. He has brought forth extensive teachings about the mystical path, many of them available for free on his websites: *www.askrealjesus.com, www.ascendedmasteranswers.com, www.ascendedmasterlight.com* and *www.transcendencetoolbox.com*. For personal information, visit Kim at *www.KimMichaels.info*.